MASTERTHINKER'S HANDBOOK
A GUIDE TO INNOVATIVE THINKING

EDWARD DE BONO

Dr. Edward de Bono dedicated his life to teaching thinking as a skill. He designed thinking tools to apply in the practical world. Born in Malta, Dr. de Bono received his initial education at St Edward's College, Malta, and the Royal University of Malta, where he achieved a degree in medicine. Then as a Rhodes Scholar at Christchurch, Oxford, where he gained a degree in psychology and physiology and a D.Phil. in medicine. He received a Phd from Cambridge, a DDes from the Royal Melbourne Institute of Technology, and a LLD from Dundee. He had faculty appointments at the universities of Oxford, Cambridge, London and Harvard.

He became interested in the nature and teaching of thinking while working in medical research investigating the self-organising nature of physiological systems. This led to his description of the behaviour of the mind as a self-organising system, (see his book *Mechanism of Mind*) and his interest in the development of lateral thinking to change perception.

Dr. de Bono originated many thinking methods that are widely used today. He originated the phrase Lateral Thinking—which has an entry in the Oxford English Dictionary. He described Parallel Thinking, also known as the Six Thinking Hats® method as an alternative to argument.

He has written over 60 books and programmes, with translations into 43 languages, has been invited to lecture in 58 countries and has made three television series. His ideas have been sought by governments, not for profit organisations and many of the leading corporations in the world, such as IBM, Boeing, BT (UK), Nokia (Finland), Mondadori (Italy), Siemens (Germany), 3M (Germany), NTT (Japan), GM, Kraft, Nestle, Du Pont, Prudential, Shell, Bosch (Germany), Goldman Sachs, Ernst & Young and many others. The global consultancy, Accenture, chose him as one of the fifty most influential business thinkers.

First published in the USA by the International Center for Creative Thinking 1985
Published by Penguin Books 1990

The content of this book may not be used in training programs except under the supervision of an authorized and certified de Bono® Trainer.

This revised edition is published by Edward de Bono Ltd t/a de Bono

First Floor, Templeback, 10 Temple Back, Bristol, BS1 6FL

© 2022. Edward de Bono Ltd. www.debono.com

ISBN: 978-1-4716-9079-2

Revised by Caspar and Josiah de Bono

CONTENTS

FOREWORD

The main difficulty with thinking is confusion. We try to do too much in our minds at once. We need some simple way of paying attention to one thing at a time. In this way we can build up a sort of map. With such a map we know where we are. We can then take appropriate action.

In this book I put forward a new framework which allows a thinker to direct his or her attention to one aspect of a matter at a time. This framework is useful in both reactive thinking (when something is put in front of you) and also in active thinking (when you have to generate the material).

I am very conscious that there are many elaborate schemes for thinking. These are often complex. They look nice in a book. But, very few people can actually remember all the steps, so the schemes tend to remain in the books rather than enter into daily use. That is why my specific purpose in putting forward the framework in this book has been to aim for something that is very simple, very easy to remember, and very easy to use.

I have chosen the 'body' as the framework because we always carry our bodies around with us. It turns out that this analogy of the human body (bones, muscle, nerves, fat) is also a most useful way of looking at thinking. What are the bones of this situation? Where is the muscle in this thinking?

My many years of experience in teaching thinking skills have convinced me that simple frameworks used effectively can be very powerful. The framework put forward in this book can be used to guide your own thinking or it can be used to focus the thinking of others.

WHAT IS A MASTER THINKER?

A master carpenter is someone who has mastered the art and craft of carpentry.

A master carpenter has at his or her fingertips the skills needed to carry out *any* carpentry task. Such a carpenter decides to do something and then sets out to do it with the confidence that arises from knowing what you need to do and how to do it.

The master carpenter has mastered the skills of carpentry. The masterthinker is someone who has mastered the skill of thinking. Thinking is a skill like any other. You can master it, just as you can master the skills of carpentry or skiing, music, or mathematics.

Far too many people believe that thinking is a matter of intelligence: If you are intelligent you will automatically be a good thinker. This is not so. In fact, many intelligent people are *poor thinkers* because they fall into the 'intelligence trap' which I shall describe later. On the other hand many people who do not have the highest IQs can become skilled thinkers—provided they set their minds to it.

If we treat thinking as a skill then we can improve thinking just as we can improve any skill through attention and practice.

THE MASTERTHINKER is someone who has developed thinking skill to a high degree. Such a masterthinker is able to direct his or her thinking to any subject whatsoever—just as that master carpenter can tackle any carpentry task.
The masterthinker has command of the tools and methods of thinking. He or she knows what to do, when to do it and how to do it. The result is confidence and effectiveness. The masterthinker sets out to do something and *knows* that at the end there will be a useful output: The problem will be solved. The plan will be made. The design will be completed. The decision will be finalized.

THE MASTERTHINKER is not concerned with proving himself or herself right and the other person wrong. The masterthinker explores the matter in an objective manner. The masterthinker is always prepared to admit when he or she is wrong. The master thinker is prepared to admit dissatisfaction with the thinking that has taken place - even when it is his or her own thinking. The masterthinker knows that the thinking is always more important than the thinker. The masterthinker is confident but never conceited. Thinking is a skill that can always be improved.

THE MASTERTHINKER is constructive rather than destructive. He or she is interested in working things out and in making things happen. The masterthinker is cooperative and can work with others in a positive sharing of thinking.

THE MASTERTHINKER knows that human emotions, human feelings, and human values are an essential part of thinking and uses them to make decisions and choices. The masterthinker is a human being not a computer.

THE MASTERTHINKER knows that thinking is the ultimate human resource and that the future of the world depends on our skilled use of that resource.

How To
Become
A
Master
Thinker

If you really want to become a masterthinker then there are a number of deliberate steps that you must take. I have listed these steps below.

STEP 1

You have to *want* to become a masterthinker.

That sounds obvious - but it is not. Very few people really want to become masterthinkers. Most people believe that their thinking is so good that there is nothing they need to do about it. They also feel that there is nothing that anyone could teach them. There is a great deal of complacency about thinking. Then there are those people who are only interested in winning arguments and proving that they are right. For them, thinking is just an extension of their ego. Such people do not want to become masterthinkers because a masterthinker must use thinking in an objective fashion - even when it means admitting that you are wrong.

STEP 2

You have to *focus* on thinking.

Now this is very difficult. We breathe, we walk, we talk and we think. But we do not really focus on these activities. They just happen as we go along. We do not need to be conscious of every step we take and of every breath we breathe. In the same way we use thinking as we go about our daily business. We do not stop to consider what we are doing. We do not actually focus on our thinking - it just seems to be there. In order to become a masterthinker you do have to focus on your thinking. You must watch yourself thinking and watch others thinking. Thinking must become an area of interest and, then a skill area. At the beginning this may seem awkward and unnatural but quite soon it becomes enjoyable. Thinking can be fun as well as useful.

STEP 3

You have to *set aside some time* for thinking.

We spend most of our time just reacting to information that is put in front of us: at school, on television, in newspapers and magazines, and in our conversations. Of course, all this does involve some thinking - but not very much. Usually we just let the information pour into us and we hope that it adds up to something in the end. How often do you say to yourself: "I am going to spend some time thinking about this?" People do not like thinking because it seems complicated and unproductive. We just seem to get ourselves into knots. As we develop skill at thinking it gets easier and more enjoyable. This is no different from learning to swim, ski or ride a bicycle. They all seem awkward at first. You have to want to keep going.

STEP 4

You have to have *some thinking techniques.*

You can order someone to 'think'. That person might try very hard - but not much will happen. You can order yourself to 'think' but not very much will happen. Effort alone is not enough. We need thinking techniques and methods. It is when we apply these with skill and effort that we get results.

The famous American philosopher William James once said that for most people "thinking was just a re-arrangement of their prejudices". This is quite a good description of what normally passes for thinking. Usually there is no more than a sort of active daydream in which we muse about the situation in the hope that we can spot a solution or course of action. At other times we use "point to point thinking" which means that we move along from one obvious point to the next, ignoring all the important routes along the way. The purpose of this handbook is to provide a set of techniques for thinking. As you go through the book you will find that you are asked to use different frameworks and techniques. There is always something to do, some thinking task to be carried out. In this way thinking becomes a step-by-step process. We take one step after another. This is very different from drifting about and hoping we come across something useful. When you have learned how to use the techniques then you will know what to do when you give yourself the order to 'think about something'. When you are really skilled in the use of the tools then you will be a masterthinker.

STEP 5

You have to *practice* your thinking.

Understanding the game of tennis is quite different from getting onto the court and playing a good game. Exactly the same applies to skiing, cooking, playing the piano, or writing computer programs. Skills have to be practiced. The more you practice a skill the better you will be able to use that skill. There is no substitute for practice. If you want to be a masterthinker you will have to practice the thinking skills set out in this handbook. The techniques set out in this book are easy to understand but only practice can give you the skill required to use them effectively. From practice comes fluency and confidence. Fluency means that you can use a technique rapidly and with ease. Confidence means that you have mastered the technique and can apply it wherever you like. Confidence also means that you know that you will get some result at the end.

It Is Up To You

If you want to become a masterthinker those are the five steps you have to take. You will need to keep reminding yourself of them. Each step is open to anyone. The steps are easy enough but they do require some effort. Athletes have to keep practicing even though they know how to run or jump. What I mean is that becoming a masterthinker is more a matter of will than of intelligence.

You will not become a masterthinker in just one jump. You will gradually get better and better at thinking. You should watch your progress and take pride in your increasing skill.

I wish you luck! The world needs all the thinkers it can get.

The Intelligence Trap

You set a bear trap to catch bears. You set an elephant trap to catch elephants. You use a mouse trap to catch mice. The intelligence trap is the trap that intelligent people sometimes set for themselves.

Why do you need to know about this intelligence trap? Well, you may be a highly intelligent person and you may already be caught in the trap. As I mentioned earlier you may consider yourself so intelligent that you feel you do not need to learn anything about thinking. Once you learn about the intelligence trap you will see that intelligence and thinking are not the same thing.

I often use the analogy of a motor car. Innate intelligence corresponds to the power of the engine and the excellence of the suspension. Thinking skill corresponds to the skill of the car driver. A powerful car may be badly driven and a more humble car may be driven very well. Intelligence represents the innate potential of the mind. The operating skill with which the mind is used is called thinking. We may not be able to do much about our innate intelligence, but we can improve our thinking skills if we make the effort.

It may be that you do not consider yourself very intelligent, but that you have to deal with intelligent people from time to time. You may feel overwhelmed by their intelligence and confuse this for thinking skill. So it could be useful to learn about the intelligence trap.

A highly intelligent person will often take a certain view on a subject and then use his or her thinking just to support that view. This will be done with arguments that make a great deal of sense. But the more able a thinker is to support a point of view the less inclined is that thinker actually to explore the subject. Since the original point of view may be based on prejudice or habit, this failure to explore the subject is bad thinking. The ability to support a particular point of view never removes the necessity to look for other points of view. By choosing our values and our perceptions it is usually possible to construct support for almost any view we like. The only protection we have against fooling ourselves is the ability to explore other views. In the end we may choose to come back to our first view but this is *after* exploring other views. So we sometimes find that the intelligent person is trapped into one point of view by his or her ability to defend that view.

Highly intelligent people are often inclined towards negative thinking. This is because they know that they are clever and they want to get a sense of achievement from that cleverness; the quickest form of achievement is to criticize someone else and prove that other person wrong. This is an immediate and complete achievement that makes one feel superior to the other person. To put forward a constructive idea is less satisfactory because you have achieved nothing until you can actually show that the idea works - and that can take time - unless it is a mathematical problem for which you can demonstrate the answer. Negative thinking is, of course, an important part of thinking but it is never enough by itself. You cannot grow a garden just by wielding the shears.

Intelligent people who are not masterthinkers do not like being wrong. Their ego and sense of personal worth has been built around their intelligence so it becomes very difficult to admit an error. This means that such people do all they can to avoid admitting an error. This makes for inefficient thinking. A masterthinker admits an error at once since his or her concern is for objective thinking. The fear of making a mistake keeps some intelligent people from putting forward speculative or creative ideas because these might turn out to be wrong. Such people do not like taking risks with their thinking. Taking risks is at times a necessary part of thinking.

Because an intelligent person's mind works very quickly such a person may jump to conclusions very rapidly. At times this can be useful. At other times it may be dangerous. A slower thinker may need to take in more information before jumping to a conclusion and so may actually come to a better conclusion.

Perhaps the biggest danger is that many highly intelligent people (especially when young) tend to be very arrogant about their thinking. This is unfortunate since there are no grounds for arrogance about thinking at any time.

I want to make it clear that not all intelligent people are caught in the intelligence trap. Nevertheless the danger is there. If you are driving a powerful car you have to be even more careful as a driver than someone driving a less powerful car. So the intelligent thinker may have to pay even more attention to thinking skills. Certainly, he or she should not assume that being intelligent is enough.

An intelligent person going through this book may find some of the techniques and exercises quite easy to do. In that case that person should do them superbly well.

Active Thinking and Reactive Thinking

Active thinking takes place when you need to take action. The purpose of your thinking is to work out what action to take. You may have to decide where you are going to go on vacation. You may have to plan that vacation. A car breaks down and you have to think how to get it going again. You want to paint the ceiling of the kitchen but you do not have a ladder: What can you do? You may be going to set up your own business or you may be going to buy someone else's business - so you are going to need a lot of help from your thinking. As a manufacturer of pens you find that your prices are too high and your customers are leaving you to buy more cheaply from your competitor: What are you going to do? Someone has told a lie about you to your mother: How can you prove this - and how can you stop that person from telling more lies? You are offered a job and have to decide whether to take it or not. All of these are situations calling for active thinking.

In active thinking - sometimes called pro-active thinking -all the facts are not right there in front of you. You have to decide what facts you need and where you will find them. For example, if you are choosing a career, it is up to you to decide what information you need. You may decide you ought to talk to someone who is following that career. If you are opening a hot dog stand, you must find out what the market might be.

In many ways *reactive* thinking is much easier. Something is put in front of you and you are asked to react to it. It may be a page in a book, a sheet of paper or a program on television. What do you think about it?

In school most of the thinking that takes place is of the reactive type. As soon as someone leaves school then most of the thinking has to be of the active type: Any initiative, plan or decision is going to have to be worked out in the future.

In reactive thinking the thinker is usually being asked one of the following questions:

Do you understand this?
Is this correct or is it wrong?
Can you organize or re-organize this information?
How can you use this information to answer a given question?

22

There are many times when active and reactive thinking come together. For example, a scientist may have to understand a situation before he or she can design an experiment. An investor may have to understand the state of the market before making an investment decision. In mathematics you have to understand the problem before trying to solve it. A doctor is continually having to use a mixture of reactive thinking and active thinking. This masterthinker's handbook deals with both active and reactive thinking. As you go through the handbook you will find techniques that apply equally to both types of thinking. At other times, a particular technique may be more useful in reactive thinking or the other way around.

The Thinking Techniques

Just asking someone (or yourself) to *think* is an important step in the right direction. But it is not enough. The answer will come back: How?

In this book I shall put forward a series of thinking techniques which together add up to a method. It is not the only possible method. Indeed I have put forward different methods elsewhere. This particular method is designed to be very simple in two respects:

1. It must be simple to learn and to remember.
2. It must be simple to use.

The main difficulty with thinking is that we cannot do everything at once. We need to separate different thinking tasks - and that is what I will teach you to do in this book.

The method I am going to use is called *BODY FRAME THINKING*. This makes it very easy to remember because after all you always have your body with you. For this method, we divide thinking into different aspects which correspond to different parts of the body: bones, muscle, nerves, fat, skin and health.

BONES

Bones are the basic elements or components. They are permanent and do not change. When we seek to 'pick out the bones' in a situation we look for the basic elements in that situation. There are big bones and small bones.

MUSCLE

Muscle is to do with force, power and energy. We look for the force or power in the thinking. This power can come about in different ways. For example, there may be information muscle, logic muscle or emotional muscle. The power may arise from the information being given. The power may arise from the force of the logic. The power may arise from the emotions and feelings. I discuss these and other sorts of power.

NERVES

Nerves are for connecting things and making things happen. The human body has nerve networks. So when we are carrying out the "nerves" part of thinking we actually make use of networks which we can draw upon a piece of paper. These networks show us how we proceed from one point to another. There are four basic types of network: achieving network, exploring network, analysing network and organizing network. We shall see how each one of these works. Note that the basic symbol for BFT (Body Frame Thinking) arises from the directions taken by each of these four networks.

FAT

A certain amount of fat is necessary to give the human body its attractive rounded appearance. But too much fat is unnecessary and even bad for health. In terms of thinking "fat" refers to excess unnecessary material. It can also refer to material which is interesting but is not part of the main message of what is being thought about.

SKIN

Skin is our appearance. We present ourselves to others through our skin. Skin forms our interface with the world of vision. In terms of thinking, "skin" refers to the presentation of our thinking. It is not enough just to think. It is not even enough just to get the right answer. In most cases we have to present the results of our thinking to others. Skin refers to the presentation and communication aspect of thinking.

HEALTH

The most important thing is that the body should be healthy. In the BFT method "health" refers to the 'evaluation' of the results of thinking. Is the outcome sound? Is the outcome healthy? What is the value of the outcome? Is the outcome dangerous? Is the outcome weak?

SUMMARY

So in the BFT method all we need to remember are six headings: bones, muscle, nerves, fat, skin, and health. In practice the three major headings are bone, muscle, and nerves.

Bones

What are the *bones* of this situation?

Pick out the *bones* of this problem?

I see the following as the *bones* of the matter. . .
If you had X-ray eyes, you would see everyone's *bones*. In a sense the *bones* are the key elements around which everything else is organized.

When ancient tombs are opened, the skull and *bones* are found lying there. All else has long since gone.

Bones are basic.

So when we set out to look for the *bones* in any situation we look for the basic ingredients of the situation, the key elements.

What are the *bones* of a chair? The seat, the back, the legs. We could also add comfort because *bones* does not only apply to physical parts.

It should be remembered that when we pick out the *bones* in a situation we always do so from our own point of view. For example, if you were a manufacturer making and selling chairs then the *bones* would include: price of production, selling price, profit, and customer appeal.

What are the *bones* of a school? Pupils, teachers, educational materials, teaching, and buildings.

What are the *bones* of a kitchen? A stove, a refrigerator, a working surface, garbage can, storage cupboards, kitchen sink. We should probably include food. There are kitchens without food (for example in newly built apartments where the kitchen is still a kitchen even though it has never been used) but usually kitchens have food in them.

What are the *bones* of a door? The doorway, the door itself, the hinges and the door handle. What about opening and closing? Yes, those are among the *bones*.

What are the *bones* of a pencil? Slim wooden rod, graphite down the centre, sharpened at one end, used for writing.

EXERCISE:

*Note down the 'bones' of each of
the following items:*

*a supermarket
a book
a dog
a telephone
a smile
a soda bottle*

It must be obvious by now that the *bones* of an object are quite similar to the description or definition of that object.

The effort to pick out the bones of a situation is not, of course, limited to objects but applies to any situation at all that we need to think about.

A young man is caught stealing a pair of jeans from a shop. What are the bones of this situation?

The young man; the jeans; the shop owner; the store detective; the police; the young man's fear; the store owner's anger.

EXERCISE –

Pick out the bones for each of the following situations –

a businessman tries to decide which personal computer to buy

a young woman drives her car into the back of a taxi cab

a friend invites you to a party

a friend does not invite you to his birthday party

The simplest way to pick out the bones is to use the question: *What are the things we need to think about in this situation*? Here, we call them "bones" but we could call them factors, elements, ingredients, features, etc.

Once you have grasped the general principle of trying to pick out the *bones* in a situation, you can move on to the next step. This is concerned with *big bones* and *small bones.*

BIG BONES, SMALL BONES

The human body contains some big bones such as the thigh bone (the femur) and the upper arm bone the (humerus). The pelvic bone is also pretty big. Then there are the small bones. The spine is made up of a number of small bones (vertebrae) arranged as a sort of chain with cartilage between them. The hand and the foot are made up of many small bones arranged in a special way for proper functioning. The ribs are what we might call middle sized bones.

In exactly the same way there are some *bones* in a situation that are much more important than others. These are the *major bones or big bones*. These big bones do not have to be big in size. For example, if you are locked out of your house, the front door key is a *big bone* even though it is rather small in size. Similarly a bullet that injures someone is a *big bone* even though the size of the bullet is small. In the thinking idiom 'big' refers to importance.

When we look for the big bones we look for the major elements. In an automobile, the engine is a big bone. So are the wheels and the steering wheel. The air conditioning and the upholstery are not.

With this concept of big bones and small bones we introduce the idea of priorities. Some things are more important than others. There are key elements in a situation and then there are other elements. To overlook a key element could be a serious mistake. To overlook some of the less important elements may not matter so much.

The fire engine races to a house that is on fire. What are the *big bones* in this situation? People to be rescued; water to put out the fire; action to keep the fire from spreading; safety of fire fighters; putting out the fire. We could have put it more simply: Saving of human lives and limiting damage.

It is perfectly in order to use a broad term that can cover several other terms. For example the term 'human lives' covers both the need to rescue people and the safety of the firemen. It is best to put down the individual *big bones* first and then to find a *bigger bone.* You also need to be very careful that your broad term is not so broad that it covers everything but indicates nothing. For instance, if you had said that the *big bone* was for the firemen to do their job properly that does cover everything, but does not tell us what needs thinking about.

EXERCISE -

Pick out the big bones in the following situations –

a bank

an airline

fire alarm systems

swimming

cartoon characters

Picking out the big bones in any situation is one of the most important thinking skills. I would go so far as to say that you cannot be a thinker unless you become very good at picking out the big bones of any situation. If we did not use the term 'big bones' then we would be talking about picking out the *fundamentals.* I prefer the term 'big bones' because it is more descriptive and it also fits in with the total thinking framework (which will include 'muscles', 'nerves' etc.).

Note that when you are thinking about something you *do not* pick out all the bones first and then divide them into big bones and small bones. What you do is to make an effort to pick out the big bones *first* and then you look around for the smaller bones.

Suppose you were thinking of setting up a mobile hot dog stand as a way of earning a living. Pick out the big bones in this situation. If you wish, pause at this point and jot down your ideas before reading on.

Your answer might look something like the following:

Profit: This is very important because without a profit you would not earn a living. So it is a big bone that you must pick out so that you can then think about it - and do your calculations.

Customers: If there are no customers you do not have a business. So you have to think about customers as a big bone. This will affect your pricing and your location: Where do you set up your stand?

Equipment: Your means of producing the hot dogs. Can you afford to buy it? Could you rent it? What do you need?

Supplies: Frankfurters, buns, napkins, etc. Where are you going to get them? How good are they? What will they cost?

There are two other big bones you might have picked out. One of these is *advertising*. How are you going to let people know about your stand and your quality? You might think of taking up a franchise in order to ensure quality. The other big bone is *testing*. Is there any way you could test out the idea before committing yourself fully? Could you borrow a hot dog stand and try things out for a couple of weeks?

In this particular example the small bones might have included such things as: name, method of getting about, clothes you wear, details of what you serve, time of operation. All of these are important, but they are less important than the *big bones*. If you treat everything as equally important then you can never get to focus your thinking on the most important things.

You may have spotted that I left out a rather big bone. This is the matter of finance or capital: You need money to get your equipment, to obtain supplies and to live on until you get going. If you already have such money, then it may not be a big bone. If you do not, then certainly it should be there among the big bones. Even so, profit and customers come first. If there is no profit or there are no customers, then there is no business so you do not have to concern yourself with raising money. On the other hand if there is good profit and enough customers, it becomes much easier to borrow the money or take in a partner.

CHECK-LIST

A check-list is a useful way of jogging our minds when we set out to pick out the bones in a situation. So here is a simple checklist.

People: Who are the people involved? Who are the actors in the situation? Who are the by-standers? Who is helping you? Who is likely to oppose you? Who matters most?

Physical Parts: What hardware is involved? What objects or items are involved?

Relationships: What are the relationships of people to each other and to you? What are the interactions between the physical parts or between people and the physical parts?

Benefits: What are the benefits? What are the dangers? How do the benefits arise? Who enjoys the benefits?

Emotions and Feelings: What are your feelings? What are the feelings of the other people involved?

I want to emphasize very strongly that when we pick out the bones in a situation we are not only concerned with the physical elements. For example, you are selling a used car to someone. One of the big bones might be *suspicion.* The "customer" wonders why you are selling the car. Is there something wrong with it? Once you can focus on this, then you might be able to do something about it: Give a short guarantee.

EXERCISE -

Pick out the big bones in the following situations:

Two friends quarrel about a third person who is liked by one of the friends but not by the other.

Her parents want a girl to study the piano but she does not want to.

You find a wallet full of money in the street.

A hijacker orders the pilot to fly to Cuba.

REACTIVE THINKING

A mass of material is put in front of you. How do you make sense of it? How do you make sense of a lecture or a particular class in school?

In order to understand things we need to sort them out. How do we start to sort things out?

The first thing we need to do is to simplify things. Later in this handbook I shall introduce the concept of *fat.* It is obvious that fat is very different from the hardness of bone. You will find that the term fat applies to padding and detail. This padding and detail obscures the bone just as real life fat can hide the shape of the bones. So in reactive thinking we make a strong effort to separate the bones from the fat. This is how we simplify things. Once we get a clear view of the bone structure then our understanding of the situation can take place.

You read through the material and try to pick out the big bones. You note these down. Then you look at what you have. Does it really cover the situation? Probably not. You may have to go through it again and alter your list of bones. You may have left something out or, some of these bones might be combined into a bigger bone.

Consider the following passage:

"The unemployment rate is likely to rise because technology means that machines can do what people had to do before. One man with a ditch-digger can dig a ditch that

35

might have needed six men or more. Two men with a combine harvester can harvest a field that might have needed fifty people. The same thing is beginning to happen in offices. Word processors and computers mean that fewer typists are necessary. Information can move around electronically instead of having to be typed up and sent by mail. Of course there will be new jobs: in making the computers, in selling them, in servicing them and in operating them. But will these new jobs make up for all the lost jobs?"

Let us see what happens when we try to pick out the big bones from that passage.

Technology is clearly a big bone.

Displacing people from jobs is another big bone.

Unemployment is mentioned only once but it is implied throughout. Where will the displaced people go? Can technology create enough new jobs? This is another big bone.

If we put all these together we have:
Technology displaces people from jobs and if technology does not create enough new jobs, then unemployment will rise.

That is a simple exercise. But there is also another layer of meaning in that passage. This is centred on the phrase "beginning to happen in the office. " We can pick this out as a key phrase. This makes it a big bone (but of a different sort - as I shall explain shortly). There is a suggestion that in the past we have coped with technology like ditch-digger machines and combined harvesters. Can we cope if automation comes to the office?
Perhaps - because people have shifted into offices.

There are two types of big bone. One type is the 'broad point' that covers and summarizes many aspects. In this sense 'people displacing' is a broad point that covers much of what is written in the passage.

The other type of big bone is a 'key point' or 'crucial point'. This may not cover anything except itself. Yet it should be noted as a big bone because it is so important. It is central and on it may depend much of the sense of what is written. So the phrase 'beginning to happen in the office' is a big bone of this second type. A hinge is small in size but the whole door pivots on it. Without the hinge there would be no door.

Consider the following passage:

"The research laboratory came up with a new type of candy that looked like little red granules. When you put some on your tongue they fizzed and popped and crackled. It was as if your mouth were filled with a miniature fireworks display. There was a flavour too, probably strawberry, but it was the sensation that was so unusual. The granules came to be called pop rocks. The problem was to test them. How would youngsters respond to them? They were certainly new. But what would happen when the novelty wore off? It was not any use asking anyone because no one can tell how soon he or she will tire of something. Should the company go ahead and produce quantities of the stuff or test it thoroughly and risk missing out on the novelty? These were difficult questions."

Novelty is clearly a big bone.

So are the marketing problem and instant appeal.

If we put these together we have summarized the problem: How to market a novel product with instant appeal.

The key type of big bone is *boredom.* The possibility of boredom is what is really causing the problem. The summary now becomes: A novel product with instant appeal but with a marketing problem—the possibility of boredom.

I do not want to suggest that on every occasion there are both the key type of big bone and the broad cover type. The broad cover type is always there because these big bones give the gist of the material. The key type may or may not be present. There may also be more than one key point.

Bones :
Summary

The buffet table is full of delicious foods: meats, vegetables, breads and fruits. You stand there, plate in hand, wondering where to start. You cannot load everything on your plate at once. You have to pick out what you like.
You have to focus on one thing at a time. Thinking is very much the same.
We can think of something as a whole just as you can look at the buffet table as a whole. But in order to do something about it, we have to start focusing on individual items. We can then think about these items one at a time.

Bones are the basic structural elements in a human body. So we use the term *bones* as the basic structural elements in what we are thinking about. The process of "picking out the *bones* of the situation" means picking out the basic elements.

BIG BONES

These are the *most important* elements. To pick out the big bones we try to find the most important elements. We shall see later that there are two types of big bone: broad type and key type.

SMALL BONES

The small bones are the other elements or factors that we have to think about. It is important that we do think about these as well but small bones are not as important as the big bones. Sometimes the small bones are grouped together to create some larger element - just as many small bones create a hand.

BIG BONES (BROAD TYPE)

Here we are looking for the main elements. This means that we can often put several things together under a broad heading. This broad heading becomes a big bone (broad type). It is a sort of summary of elements. For example, if you were setting up a small business one of the big bones for consideration would be 'finance'. This broad term covers the needs and ways of getting the money.

BIG BONES (KEY TYPE)

This is a bone that is very important - so important that it is a key to the whole situation. For example, in thinking of setting up a small business a key type of big bone might be 'health'. If your health is poor you may not want to start on a venture you cannot sustain.

Active thinking:

Active thinking takes place when we list all the things we need to think about to solve a problem or make a decision. We have to find these things. They are not written out for us. We deliberately use our thinking to pick out the big bones and then we continue thinking to pick out all the other bones that need thinking about. Anything that we ought to give some thought to must be on our list of the bones of the situation.

Reactive Thinking:

Reactive thinking is simply reacting to something that is put in front of us.
It may be a report, a news article, a television program, or a teacher's explanation. We look through the material for the big bones (broad type) first. Then we look for the big bones (key type). Then we look for the other bones. If you are asked to write a report on some material or to produce an essay, you might want to lay out the bones first and then to decide how you are going to put them together. This will give you structure and it will also give you a focus for your thinking - you know at each moment what you are thinking about.

Phrases:

The sort of instructions that you might give yourself or to others are indicated below:

I want to pick out the bones of this situation.
What do you see as the bones of this matter?
Let us pick out the big bones and focus upon them.
There is a mass of material here, what are the bones of it?
Give me the bones of it, please. Just the bones.
What are the bones of this problem?
Before we make a plan we should list the bones.
I see these as the big bones.
Make a list of the big bones

SKILL

The process of picking out the bones of a situation is not difficult to understand. But it is quite difficult to do really well. Therefore, you will need to practice it as much as you can. If you cannot get the bones right, then the rest of your thinking will be ineffective.

41

Muscle

The two tough looking truck drivers sit down at the small table. Everyone gathers around. Each of the drivers rests his elbow on the table and then they clasp hands. The arm wrestling match has begun. The strain shows on the face of each driver as he strives to bend the forearm of his opponent back to the table. It is clear that each man is using the maximum amount of muscle of which he is capable.

The setting is the Olympic stadium and the event is women's javelin throwing. In turn each woman grasps the javelin and breaks into a run that ends with a few long steps. At the end of these, the javelin is hurled high into the air with the full force of the woman's muscle behind it.

We all know what is meant by *muscle*. By muscle we mean force and power. It is our muscles, attached to our bones, that enable us to walk, run, lift, carry or indeed to move at all. Should our muscles become paralyzed or very weak we would be incapable of moving at all.

So the term *muscle* is going to refer to force or power.

We all know the expression: "What is the force of this argument?"

In the business world 'market muscle' refers to the ability of an organization to distribute and sell something. The mighty IBM corporation was late in getting started with its personal computer. At last it entered the market with the IBM PC. The name and market muscle of IBM soon ensured that the IBM PC captured up to 30 percent of the market.

Just as *bones* referred to the basic elements in a thinking situation, so *muscle* refers to the force or power of the thinking. A masterthinker tries to pick out and identify this force.

PURPOSE

A person in a wild frenzy may hit out in all directions with no clear purpose for the use of his or her muscles. In a seizure a person's muscles may tense and jerk, again without any defined purpose. In general, however, there is always a *purpose* for the use of our muscles. We use our muscles to achieve something. Each of the two truck drivers was using his muscles to achieve victory. The javelin throwers were using their muscles to hurl the javelin further than their competitors. IBM used its market muscle to establish its PC in the market and to sell as many as possible.

We may take it that force or muscle is generally used for a purpose. So in discussing *muscle* we first have to take a look at purpose. The *force* of an argument is used to win that argument. The power of a logical sequence is directed towards proving something. The power of an emotional appeal is directed towards persuading people.

ACTIVE THINKING

You are setting out to do something. You are using your thinking to achieve that thing. Please define as clearly as you can what you want to achieve. What is the purpose of your thinking? All active thinking has a purpose. This may be hidden, vague or clearly defined. A masterthinker will make a strong effort to define his or her purpose as clearly as possible.

If you do not know where you are going, why should you expect to get there.

We use a lot of different words to describe what we want to do:

objective

goal

target

aim

purpose

intention

desire

You could set out to show how each of these is different and has a proper place in the English language. For our purpose here that would only be confusing because we would then need to remember the exact meaning of each of the terms. For that reason I intend to use just two: purpose and objective.
    What is the purpose of our thinking?
    What objective do we want to reach?

The masterthinker asks himself or herself these questions quite often. The more clearly you know where you are going, the more effective will be your thinking.

There is a simple and very powerful question which summarizes this sense of purpose in thinking. The question is:

What do we want to have at the end of our thinking'?

In other words, what do we want to end up with?

We might want to end up with a number of different things: a solution to a problem, a plan of action, a decision or choice, a new invention, a defined opportunity, a negotiated settlement to a dispute the identity of the criminal, a persuasive argument.

Once you have defined your purpose then you can use the muscle of your thinking to achieve that purpose.

EXERCISE

For each of the following situations, spell out what you think the purpose of the thinker might be. What does the person involved want to end up with?

The owner of a drug store finds that many items are being stolen from his store. He suspects a group of boys who are often in the store.

A girl hears that a friend of hers has been spreading rumours about her.

A motor car breaks down on a lonely road in the middle of the night. The temperature is below freezing.

An entrepreneur is looking for a name for a new chain of fast food restaurants that are going to sell curried food.

As you go through this exercise you will find that it is not quite as easy as it seems. It is clear enough what each of the people might want, but when we come to spell it out there seem to be several possible purposes at the same time.

For example, we might say that the purpose of the drug store owner is to "prevent any further losses." We might also have said that his purpose was "to catch and punish the thieves. " Or we could have said that his purpose was "to prove that the boys were doing it." You might say that it does not matter how the purpose is defined. But it does matter.

If the owner's purpose is revenge or justice then he might think about setting a trap for the youngsters (or any other thief). If his purpose is to prevent any further losses, then he might warn the youngsters specifically or perhaps set up mirrors that would enable him to see more of the store.

You could, of course, say that the drugstore owner has two purposes: to prevent further losses and to punish the past thieves.

With the girl who hears her friend has been spreading rumours we might find a range of objectives:

> to find out if it is true
> to stop it
> to punish the friend (if it is true)
> to find out what is really happening (if it is not true)
> to counteract the rumours

With the car that breaks down we might find the following range of objectives:
> to get the car going again
> to keep alive in the cold temperature
> to get some help
> to go somewhere warmer

We should note that within each of these objectives there will be sub-objectives. For example, the overall objective might be to get the car going again. Within this would be the objective to "find out what was wrong." Once this was done then the objective would be "to put things right. " In a particular case this might require a piece of wire. So the next sub-objective might be "to find a piece of wire."

For the entrepreneur looking for a name for a chain of fast food restaurants we could say that his objective was "to find a suitable name." As an overall objective this is fine but within that there are a number of other objectives: to find a name that is catchy and easy to remember to find a name that indicates what kind of food is being sold to check that the name is not already in use

Overall objectives:
The overall objective is what we are trying to reach in the end. For example, we might want to be heading North. It is always best to start by trying to define the overall objective.

Sub-objectives:
These are objectives which we have to achieve in order to reach the overall objective. For example, in order to head North, we might actually have to turn South for a short while at a particular point. If we are taking a long trip, then the ultimate destination is our overall objective but the various towns along the route become sub-objectives.

Parallel objectives:
This means that there are several objectives. For example, an author might say: I want to make a lot of money and I want to be famous. There is no harm in being greedy so long as you remember that it is much more difficult to achieve several objectives at the same time.

Alternative objectives:
This means that we set out different objectives so that if we cannot achieve one, then we might achieve another. For example, a corporation buys a small business in a new field and says: "If we cannot make a go of this, at least it will be a learning experience in this new field. " A gambler might say: "If I win, that is fine; if not, I shall enjoy the excitement of playing. "

Hierarchy of objectives:
This is very important. We put down all the objectives and then arrange them in order of importance with the most important objective at the top of the list. For example in the broken-down car example, the most important objective is "to stay alive.'' Note that the most important objective does not mean the one that has to be tackled first. The first thing to do would be to try to re-start the car.

All these different types of objective are important in active thinking.

The important thing to do is to put down the possible objectives in any situation. This is what *you actually try to do*. When you have listed them, then you may find that you have parallel objectives or alternative objectives or a hierarchy of objectives. You may even find that you have overall objectives and sub-objectives.

In practice you do two things:
1. List the objectives.
2. Look at your list and change it if you wish.

Changing the list may mean putting things in order of importance or dropping out some objectives.

The relationship between overall objectives and sub-objectives is rather more active. If you have an overall objective, you may find that you have to break it down into sub-objectives in order to do any further thinking about it - and especially in order to take action. At other times you may find that you have just listed objectives which are really sub-objectives and then you have to set about finding the overall objective. For instance, the overall objective for buying a new car might be to keep up with your neighbour.

EXERCISE

Spell out the objectives which you would have if you were trying to do each of the following things:

Find someone to go on a skiing vacation with you.
Buy a used car.
Take up photography as a hobby.
Raise money for African famine relief.
Train a parrot to talk.

REACTIVE THINKING

There is a fundamental difference between the purposes of active and reactive thinking. You know what is in your mind. You can spell out what you are trying to achieve. It may take a little effort but in the end you can define the purpose of your thinking. With reactive thinking, you can only *guess* at the purpose of what is happening. You look at some written material and guess at the intention of the writer. You may make a pretty good guess or the purpose may be very clear from the writing itself - nevertheless it remains a guess. You may look at some happening and guess at the intention behind it.

A girl changes her hair style to 'punk' style. What is the purpose? Perhaps she was just bored. Perhaps she wanted to show her boyfriend that she had spirit. Perhaps she wanted to shock her parents. Perhaps she wanted to keep up with her friends. Perhaps she wanted to preserve her reputation for being in tune with the latest fashion. You could ask the girl but still might not get the right answer.

So in reactive thinking we really ought to talk about 'possible purpose' or 'apparent purpose'.

Because we cannot be sure of the actual purpose we need to think of a number of possibilities. Once we can think of these possibilities, then we can set about checking them out.

It should always be remembered that in reactive thinking the sense of purpose may be less strong than it is in active thinking where we are actually trying to do something.

'Description' is a valid purpose for an author of written material. The author may simply be trying to describe what he or she sees or has experienced.
This is supposed to be the purpose of newspaper reporters or television journalists. Often, however, we can detect that the author is trying to persuade us of something or trying to get us to see something in a particular way.

49

When confronted with presented material we can ask ourselves a simple question:

What is the originator of the material trying to get us to feel or believe?

EXERCISE -

Spell out the possible purposes behind each of the following situations:

Someone you have always disliked suddenly makes a great effort to be friendly towards you.
The cat stops eating its food, but does not lose weight.
In a magazine article the writer claims he has met and talked to a little green spaceman.
There is a lot of increased police activity in your neighbourhood.
A politician makes a speech saying that the unemployment rate for teenagers is much too high.
The President of the United States agrees to meet the leader of the Soviet Union.

EXERCISE -

What do you think is the purpose of the writer of the following piece:

"The Japanese are said to score ten points higher than Caucasians in IQ tests. They seem to be more disciplined and to work much harder. The export performance of Japan is such that there is a positive trade balance with most of the rest of the world - except perhaps as regards the supply of oil and some raw materials. There are no more radios made in the U.S.A. Japanese cars are taking over more and more of the U.S. car market. Even the electronics industry is finding it harder and harder to compete with Japan. The tax system in the U.S. does not encourage savings and without savings there can be no investment in industry. Without such investment, U.S. industry is bound to fall behind Japanese industry. What is the industrial future of the U.S.A. going to be?"

Purpose and Muscle:

Once we have a clear sense of purpose then we can move on to considering muscle.

As regards active thinking we need to consider what 'muscle' we can use in order to achieve our purpose.

As regards reactive thinking we look to see what *muscle* the originator of the material is using to make his or her case.

MUSCLE

Muscle is power or force. When it comes to thinking there are many different sorts of power and it is best to consider each of these separately.

INFORMATION MUSCLE

This is the most powerful of all. If you had complete and totally reliable information on everything, then you would not need to do any thinking.

You have a ruler and you measure the piece of wood in front of you. The information is first-hand and reliable. You are travelling abroad and you have an electric plug in your hands. You can see for yourself if it fits into a socket.

Materials vary in hardness. Diamonds are extremely hard, metal is hard but not as hard as diamonds. There is hard wood like teak and softer wood like pine. There is plastic and then there is rubber. Finally we might come to wool which is very soft. So there is a scale of hardness with diamonds at one end and wool at the other. We can put information on a similar type of scale. At one end we have hard information which means that it is reliable and trustworthy. At the other end we have soft information which means it is unreliable and untrustworthy.

I have suggested that information that is in front of you and that you can check out for yourself is reliable. This is usually true, but not always so. People do have hallucinations and believe they see something which is not actually there. Witnesses at traffic accidents sometimes contradict each other. On the whole however, if you can check things out for yourself then that is hard information. Then there are things which everyone accepts as being true: Mount Everest is the highest mountain in the world; Paris is the capital of France; the Concorde can fly at twice the speed of sound. You need not have actually seen these things for yourself. Such things are usually called *common knowledge*. There have been occasions in history when *common knowledge* has turned out to be wrong: The notion that the sun moves around the earth. But for practical purposes we accept it. Hard information includes *scientific facts* - this means truths that have been tested by different scientists. It also means reliable statistics. At its best this sort of truth is very good. Unfortunately it is very easily abused. It is easy to claim that something is a scientific fact when it is not. Unless we know the details of a test or experiment, we cannot be sure that the scientist is warranted in his or her conclusion. It may not have been a fair test or the method of measurement may have been inapplicable.

Then there are beliefs. Beliefs may be held by millions of people. Does that make them true? There are many different beliefs; are they all true?

I shall discuss beliefs later, on their own. The simplest practical way to deal with them at this point is to acknowledge something as 'a belief'.

What about information provided by other people? Here we are dealing with the credibility of the other people. We must also realize that other people may be honestly mistaken. They may not be trying deliberately to deceive us - yet what they relate may be wrong. There are certain people in authority: teachers, parents, politicians, journalists, authors. Does that mean that they are more likely to be right. The answer is 'yes' for a number of reasons. They probably got to that position because they were reliable (does not apply to parents). They would quickly get a reputation for dishonesty if they were truly dishonest. They have more experience (does apply to parents). They are trying to be reliable (usually). This does not mean that people in authority are always reliable.

We must also consider *partialism*. A person may be absolutely correct in what he or she says - but that person may have left out facts. This is what is called "half-truths'. It may be true that Joe shot Jerry. But Jerry may have tried to stab Joe first.

We now have to bring in purpose. The politician is trying to persuade voters to vote for him or her. The journalist is trying to write an interesting (or sensational) story. If the person providing the information has a purpose other than *objective description,* then that information is not very hard - it does not have much muscle.

What about the information coming from ordinary people - not in authority? It may be true or untrue. The information can be honest, honest but mistaken, honest but incomplete or deliberately false. We need to make our own assessment in each case. We do this by asking the two questions:
1. Is this person in a good position to give us hard information?
2. What is the purpose of this person in giving us the information?

A person who is trying to sell you his house may give you rather incomplete information about the traffic noise in the neighbourhood. A person who is trying to sell you a cure for baldness may give you false information about its effectiveness.

Assessment of information muscle:

We can set out to assess the information muscle in situations that involve either active or reactive thinking.

In active thinking we need to see what information we have and how good it is. We also need to see what further information we need - and to consider ways of getting this.

In reactive thinking, a major part of our thinking effort is directed towards assessing the 'information muscle' of what has been put in front of us.

To assess information muscle we need to ask two questions:
1. How much information do we have?
2. How 'hard' is this information?

Taken together the quantity and quality of the information available determine the information muscle of a situation.

EXERCISE -

Assess the information muscle of the following piece:

"There was a recent report from the pilot of a Russian airliner flying inside Russia, of the sighting of a UFO. The pilot reported that this glowing green object followed his plane for some time before zooming away at unnatural speed. It is reported that radar operators reported seeing two objects on their screens. Yet there were no other planes scheduled in that area at that time. The report was put out by the official Soviet news agency and must therefore have been approved by the authorities. Some reports of UFO sightings in the U.S.A. have subsequently been shown to be hoaxes or to be caused by light planes flying under special conditions. Nevertheless there remain reports which have not been explained. In some cases the sightings have been made by a number of different people placed at different points. The fact that some sightings have been mistakes does not mean that all such sightings must be wrong. There are thousands of millions of star systems and any one of these may have its own planets. On one such planet the conditions for life might be available. Can we believe that it is only on our planet that advanced intelligent life exists ?"

53

LOGIC MUSCLE

This is the next most important type of *muscle.* With logic we seek to go from what we know to what we do not yet know. Alternatively, we seek to show that a position we hold is 'logically' based on what we do know for certain.

It should be said at once that the most perfect form of logic exists in constructed systems. When you design a game you set out the rules of that game. When you are playing the game you have to follow the logic of those rules. After all we have set them up in the first place and also chosen to play the game. For example, in playing Monopoly it is a rule of the game that you do not collect money when passing 'Go' on the way to jail.

If you set up a system of numbers and notations then it follows that $2 + 2 = 4$ in such a system. Quite often, however, the implications of what we have decided upon are not obvious. It may require a lot of thought to work things out. Yet those implications are already built into the system (or universe) we have set up.

If you draw lines which are not parallel on a plane surface then they must meet somewhere. This is a logical deduction that follows from the nature of the surface. In a three dimensional environment such lines may not meet.

So the purpose of logic is to bring out what is implicit and necessary in those things we have either constructed or accepted.

With a mathematical proof we move step-by-step according to the rules of mathematics, until we have completed the proof.

Scientific proof is much less satisfactory because we have not actually constructed the *universe.* We just try very hard to limit the variable features in a certain experimental *universe.* We can then say the following: Under exactly these circumstances an increase in A will be followed by an increase in B. We then use statistics to show that this is rather unlikely to have been produced by chance. If we conduct the experiment often enough and if other scientists find the same results, then we are inclined to say we have scientific proof that A causes an increase in B. There are well-known pitfalls in this type of proof. For example, we could show a statistical correlation between the rise in the number of refrigerators and a fall in infant deaths.
We might at once say that the possibility of keeping food chilled has reduced bacterial infection in children's' food and so has reduced infant deaths. This is indeed plausible.

We could also say that the increase in the number of refrigerators means more affluent people who can maintain better standards of hygiene and also learn more about baby care. It can also be that the more affluent society can afford more refrigerators, more doctors, more hospitals, and better medical research. This type of research is notoriously difficult because it is not possible to isolate the factors of interest as it is in a laboratory. For instance, we think we know that smoking causes lung cancer. All the evidence supports this. We might, however, need to modify this by saying that smoking causes lung cancer only in those people who have a particular enzyme defect. Or we might have to say that smoking allied with a particular virus (or other factor) causes lung cancer.

Most of the time we are dealing with what may be called *"language logic."* This means the ordinary logic that we use when speaking or writing. It usually takes the form of: *"if this is so, then this follows."* This can be modified to: *"if this and this are so, then this follows."*

The car will not start in the morning. So we go through some simple logic. If the car battery is charged then the headlights should work. The headlights work - so the battery is all right. Note that this does not work the other way around. If the headlights did not work, it would not necessarily mean the battery needed charging - the battery connection was loose. Errors of logic can lead to false conclusions. There are many excellent books on logic. I do not intend to go into details here. There are, however, some practical rules which we do need to keep in mind.

The first rule to remember is that logic can never be any better than its starting point (technically called the premise). If you start off by saying, "All women are more organized than men," and then continue to say "Therefore my wife should do the household accounts," your conclusion is no better than the strength of your starting assumption. Far too often we look at the excellence of the logical deduction and overlook the weakness of the starting point. So the first rule is to pay close attention to the starting point. Do you accept the starting point? Remember that once you have accepted the starting point you may find yourself committed to the conclusion.

The second simple rule to apply is:

Does this necessarily follow ?

Usually, in order to show that something does not *necessarily* follow, we have to *imagine* some circumstance that shows some other possibility. For example, if the car headlights did not work does that necessarily mean that the battery has run down? No, because I can imagine a loose battery connection or a blown headlight fuse or failed headlight bulbs. What about the reverse? If the headlights do light, does this mean the battery is *not* run down? We must, of course, be talking about a powerful beam not a dim light. The answer is that I cannot really imagine any circumstance in which the headlights would shine powerfully, with the engine un-started, and the battery need charging. Just possibly, I can imagine that someone has set out to fool me and has wired the headlights up to some hidden battery.

In the other example, even if all women are indeed more organized than men, does it follow that they should do the household accounts? No, because we could imagine that the women would be better employed running businesses and leaving the men to do simple things like the household accounts.

Traditional logic has to be based on words like *"all"* and *"never"* and *"cannot"*. In short it must be absolute. All parrots can learn to talk. This is a parrot, so it is worth trying to teach it to talk. As soon as we move away from the absolute then we have to use a different sort of logic.

In practice we very often need to use words like *generally, usually, on the whole, by and large.* These are not absolute because they allow for exceptions. For example, "Swans in England are usually white." This allows us the possibility of finding an occasional black swan in England. We can never proceed from such words to the absolute certainty of logic. The best we can do is to say that something is likely, probable or even just possible. Then we have to check it out in some other way.

For example we might say: "When a car does not start in the morning, it is usually due to a discharged battery." This does not prove anything, but it gets us to check out the battery first.

The assessment of logic muscle:

To do this we need to spell out the logical line that is being taken. This needs to be done in small steps. So we write down each step. Then we look to see whether the steps follow one from another and if this connection is a *necessary* one. Finally we see if the logic gets us anywhere.

In the case of the car that would not start the logic lines might have been as follows:

The usual cause of failure to start in the morning is a discharged battery. If the headlights are working the battery cannot be discharged. The headlights are working so the battery cannot be discharged.

If the headlights are working the battery cannot be discharged. The headlights are working so the battery cannot be discharged.

EXERCISE —

Put down the logic lines that you find in the following passage:

"There is increasing violence in society. Every copy of every newspaper has stories of murder, muggings, rape and every sort of violence. If there is the slightest quarrel people seem to want to shoot it out. A large part of this may be due to television. Youngsters watch over twenty hours of television a week. In that week there may be as many as 120 murders on television and numerous acts of violence. If this is what you watch, then you must come to think that this sort of behaviour is normal for society. Also in television stories the good guys or heroes use as much violence as the bad guys. They use it to deal with the bad guys, but this only serves to make violence brave and heroic. In many stories the bad guys are the police and the good guy is some independent acting as a vigilante. It is said that there is no statistical evidence that television violence increases violence in society. But this is because it would be extremely hard to measure and to prove that sort of thing. So should we not take any action unless this can be proved? Should we not follow our common-sense on such matters? If television programmers say that without violence their programs would not be interesting enough to watch, then we can turn that back to front. What about a "murder tax" of $5,000per murder in prime time - with adjusted rates for other times?

Although picking out and examining the logic lines is a very important part of reactive thinking, it is also necessary in active thinking. When you are setting out to do something you should also put down the logic lines that make you think you will be a success.

For example, you want to set up a small business to *customize* cars. Your logic lines might be as follows:
1. People want to express their individuality. In a uniform society they want visible opportunities to be different.
2. Not many people can afford to buy exotic cars like a Porsche or Lamborghini. They need a cheaper way of being different.
3. A cheaper way of being different would be to have your car painted in an exotic manner. In fact it is then even more individual than an expensive car.
4. Once we get going then the true car freaks will want real customizing jobs.
5. We will not need to advertise because every job we do will be an advertisement for us as it goes through the streets.

6. We can start slowly and build up as we go. We will get paid in advance for each job we do.

EXERCISE -

Jot down the logic lines for each of the following situations:

You and your friends want to set up a clean-out business in which you offer to clean out houses or apartments for a fee. The discarded stuff will be given to Goodwill Industries. You want to set up a shopping service for busy people or older people.

You need to be as critical of the logic lines you set up yourself as you are of those set up by other people. Remember that, in being critical, you examine the validity of each logic line and then the validity of the connection between the logic lines (does this necessarily follow?).

EXERCISE -

What is wrong with the following logic lines ?

1. There is a high rate of unemployment, especially among teenagers.
2. In some areas there are job vacancies and jobs which cannot get done.
3. Therefore, it must follow that the unemployed do not really want work.

EMOTIONAL MUSCLE

In practice this may be the most important type of muscle because it tends to be the one most often used. Emotional muscle does not have the validity of information muscle or logic muscle - and yet, in the end, it is what determines action. As a masterthinker you need to be very good at spotting emotional muscle both in others and in yourself.

This is what I feel and this is what I want you to feel.

The above statement sums up the use of emotional muscle in reactive thinking. You are reading some written material and it becomes obvious to you that the author has some strong feelings about the subject. The author expresses these feelings and seeks to persuade you to share his or her feelings. It would be fair to say that *most writing* is of this sort. Most of the time there is some message or some persuasion going on. Sometimes it may be very mild but often it is quite blatant. This is not surprising because writers are human beings who have feelings that they wish to express. For example,
I want to express the feeling that *thinking* is a good thing.

Assessing emotional muscle:

Fortunately, the assessing of emotional muscle is one of the simplest things to do.

The first thing you need to do to assess the emotional muscle of a piece of writing or a speech is to ask yourself the basic question regarding purpose: What is the author of this piece trying to do?
In most cases, the answer will be obvious and could take the following forms:

The writer is trying to show that...
The writer is trying to make the case that...
The writer is indicating that he or she does not like this subject...
The writer is obviously in favour of...

Please note that trying to make a case with information muscle or logic muscle *does not* constitute emotional muscle. Emotional muscle enters when *feelings* are used to make the case. Nevertheless when we are assessing emotional muscle, we need to spell out what we perceive to be the purpose of the material.

The second thing you need to do is to focus on the adjectives and adverbs. You can put a ring around them in written material or just note them in spoken material. Emotional muscle depends on adjectives and adverbs. This is because we have to express 'flavour' with adjectives and adverbs. I am not saying that it is impossible to use emotional muscle without an excess of adjectives or adverbs, but it is much more difficult and more rare.

Consider the following passage:

"Children are noisy, inconsiderate and demanding. They have immense egos and seem to think the world should be centred on their needs. They are extremely selfish. They are cruel but expect others to be kind to them. They enter your life and take it over. They are ungrateful for what they receive and expect it as their due. Then they leave when it suits them. But they will come back if they are in trouble and need you."

It is obvious that this is written by someone who does not like children. This dislike may be permanent or just a reaction to some temporary way in which children have disappointed the author. We can easily spot the negative adjectives: noisy, inconsiderate, demanding, immense, selfish, cruel and ungrateful. Note that emotional muscle can also be expressed without an adjective or adverb, for example: "enter your life and take it over."

59

Let us imagine the same passage written by someone who loves children.

"Children are vigorous, alive and spontaneous. They exist as beings in their own right and are not frightened of the world around them. They are their own people. They are not hypocritical but express their true feelings. They quickly become the focal point of your interest because other things seem less important. They are not subservient and they contribute with their joy and innocence. They are eager to become independent but know that they can return to the nest when they need to."

Here the adjectives include: vigorous, alive, spontaneous, not frightened, not hypocritical, true (feelings), not subservient, eager, independent.

Sometimes an *adjective* will be substituted by a phrase. For example, we might say about someone: "He has deceived us in the past and will do so again in the future." This is equivalent to saying: "He is deceitful." It is part of the assessment of emotional muscle to go through a piece attempting to substitute adjectives for some of the phrases. For instance, in the passage on children we could replace "express their true feelings" with an adjective like "sincere" or "genuine." You do, however, have to be careful and honest when substituting adjectives in this way. You must be careful not to insert your own feelings.

How valid is emotional muscle?

This is a very interesting question. As I have mentioned earlier, in the end all our choices and decisions are based on our feelings. That is as it should be because we are human beings not computers and the purpose of decisions is to serve us as humans. In spite of this ultimate importance of feelings and emotions, emotional muscle has very little validity. All emotional muscle does is to allow the writer or speaker to say, "These are my feelings on this subject." That is an exercise in self-expression. The reader or listener can take note of this but has no need at all to be persuaded by this exhibition of feelings. As a reader or listener your feelings can be aroused by information or by logic and as a result your own emotional decision may be altered. But to allow your emotions to be altered directly by the emotions of others is not part of your behaviour as a masterthinker. This sort of emotional response to emotions has led to some very inspiring moments in the history of mankind and it has also led to some of the ugliest expressions of human nature.

Most of what I have said with regard to emotional muscle has applied to reactive thinking. As a thinker you are listening to someone else or reading something that has been written. For example, whenever you are listening to a political speech it is good practice to make an effort to pick out the emotional muscle being used. As with the other aspects of thinking, emotional muscle can also apply to active thinking.

In active thinking, when you are about to undertake something, you can pause and ask yourself: "What emotional muscle am I putting into this?"
You may then find that you are embarking on some business deal out of a sense of *revenge.* Or you may find that you are motivated by *anger.* On the other hand, you may find that you are motivated by *enthusiasm* for some small aspect of the matter. For example, it is said that the backers of Broadway plays invest a lot of money because they want a chance to meet the actresses involved.

The greatest motivators for decisions are three: greed, fear and laziness. People make decisions because they are greedy, ambitious, and want more (there is nothing wrong with this). People make decisions because they are frightened of something - or they decide to do nothing because of fear. People also tend to make least-hassle decisions because they want a quiet life and are rather lazy. So whenever we are about to make a decision we should look for the *emotional muscle* attached to each of the possible choices. We can do this as follows.

For each of the possible choices we say: What is the emotional muscle attached to this particular choice?

VALUE AND BELIEF MUSCLE

I shall treat these two types of muscle together because they are interlocked. Very often our values are derived from our belief systems. For example, compassion for others often derives from Christian beliefs in the West and from other religions in the East.

Underlying values and beliefs can be expressed through logical muscle or through emotional muscle. It should be said that value muscle and belief muscle are possibly the most powerful forms of muscle. On many occasions they override both information muscle and logic muscle. The belief systems of Christian martyrs or Islamic warriors leads them to embrace death in the belief that their reward will be heaven. This is obviously contrary to unbelieving human nature.

It is my intention here to respect different value and belief systems. The role of the masterthinker is to acknowledge such systems. The thinker then seeks to spell out the contribution made by both value muscle and belief muscle to any piece of thinking.

"You have come to this conclusion because you hold these values..."

"Your perception is based on this particular belief..."

"Am I right in assuming that your decision is based on this value...?"

"At the bottom of this dispute is the clash of these two value systems."

In democratic societies, a strong value is put on individual freedom, enterprise, and expression. In centralized societies, the values are put on the general good rather than on the individual good. This means that the wellbeing of the state is of the greatest importance and then from this will flow the well-being of individuals.

In Western cultures a lot of emphasis is put on the ego and individual effort. A person acquires status and merit through his or her own efforts. In Japan, the ego is not a value source. On the contrary, value derives from how well a person *fits in* with the group or the surroundings. In some cultures, people try to stand out, in others, they try to fit in.

A sensitive person may put a high value on the feelings of others. Such a person may not like hurting or disappointing others. Another person may put a high value on efficiency. The first person may have difficulty firing someone, the second person does not.

Assessing value muscle and belief muscle:

This is not difficult. We need to ask two basic questions:

What are the underlying beliefs and values here?

In what way do these beliefs and values affect the thinking? The right word to use is *clarification* which means: let us be quite clear about the value muscle and belief muscle in this situation. Once we have clarity we can proceed.

EXERCISE -

Spell out the value muscle in the following passage:

"Supposing we found a way of overcoming the rejection problem and so

became able to do heart transplants in any patient who required one. This would mean that any patient with a defective heart would not be condemned to death but would have a new lease of life. Imagine how you would feel if you are the husband, wife, child or parent of such a patient. But each such operation would be very expensive, ranging in price perhaps from $20,000 to $50,000. Would this mean that such operations were only for the rich? Suppose, somehow, that the government made them available to everyone. Is that the best use of that money? Could that money be used more effectively to raise the standard of living of poor people? Could it be used to help starving people in Africa? Perhaps the cost of one such operation could save the lives of 300 children. Maybe we should cut down on the billions of dollars spent on rockets and defence in order to finance these heart operations. Would that make us vulnerable to an aggressor. If we were not able to defend ourselves, then our way of life might be threatened. At best, several thousand people a year would benefit from the operations but millions might be put at risk."

As with emotional muscle, much of what I have said about value muscle and belief muscle applies to reactive thinking. There is also an element which applies to active thinking.

When you are about to undertake something you can ask: What are the values here?

For example you may find that you are committing yourself to a task which will have a high reward value financially, but will mean that you spend very little time at home - so the family values suffer. Or you may find that what you are setting out to do may make money but may harm other people (for example by increasing pollution).

EXERCISE

You are running a successful restaurant that has built up a reputation for the quality of the food. In spite of the number of customers, you are not making a profit because the food costs are exceptionally high. You find that your excellent chef is running a racket. He over-orders food and then gives it to his brother who is running a restaurant in another part of town. You have evidence that this is what is happening but cannot quite prove it. What action should you take? If you lose your chef, you may not get one as good. The chef is also very temperamental and quick to take offense.

Spell out the value muscle in this situation.

HABIT MUSCLE

This may seem an unusual type of muscle but it is important. It covers continuity, cliche, inertia, and established patterns.

It is easiest to continue to do things in the same way.

A strong pressure is exerted by habit, momentum, and inertia. We can call this strong pressure or force a type of 'muscle'.

In terms of reactive thinking we come across habit muscle as cliche phrases, ideas and perceptions. This means that the writer or speaker is just repeating standard phrases and opinions without thinking about them. Elsewhere I have called these *ready-mades.*

"Do you really mean that or are you just using a standard opinion?"

That is the sort of question you can ask yourself, someone else or (in a sense) the originator of some material. You can sit listening to a talk and keep noticing *standard opinion.* These may take the form of prejudices.

Examples of this sort of thing might include: women are too emotional to be good managers, scientists are wrapped up in their work and impractical business tycoons are ruthless, the Japanese are very efficient, country people have good basic values, military spending is too high, teenagers are emotionally mixed-up, health foods are good for you, advertising is dishonest, great sports idols are great people, politicians are only out for themselves.

EXERCISE

Look at the preceding list of standard ready-made opinions and continue it with some examples of your own.

Assessing *habit muscle* is important both in reactive thinking and also in active thinking. You need to know how someone else is using the momentum of standard opinions, but you also need to assess the contribution of habit muscle to your own active thinking.

Let us look first at active thinking. You are setting out to do something and you want to assess the contribution of habit muscle to your thinking. This habit muscle can take one of three forms:

1. Have a look at your own thinking and your own plans. Are you being too conventional? Is there a different way of doing things? Should you be more creative? Should you find alternatives? Are you trapped in one way of looking at things? Note that habit muscle is the opposite of creativity.

2. In terms of what you are setting out to do, what habits are you going to try to change? Where is inertia or habit likely to be a problem for you? What resistance to change are you going to come across?

3. How can you use habit muscle for your own advantage? What existing habits, cliches or standard opinions can you tap into? If people are set in their ways can you turn that into an advantage?

This interaction between change and habit is of the greatest importance for any action thinker. It may be noble to try to change the world completely, but it is more practical to assess the points you need to change and those you need to preserve.

EXERCISE

You have invented a new sort of liquid for people to put on their breakfast cereal. It looks like milk but it is not milk. It is actually made up of finely ground nuts suspended in orange juice. It has a brown colour.

In attempting to market this new food invention list the points at which habit muscle will be working in your favour, and the points when it will be working against you.

Let us look now at reactive thinking. How do we pick out the instances of habit muscle in written material or in spoken material?

We do this in the same way as we pick out instances of emotional muscle. In written material we circle those phrases which we regard as cliches. In spoken material we mentally circle those items which we regard as *standard opinions*. We just need to make ourselves sensitive to these things and then they will become more obvious.

EXERCISE

Pick out the examples of habit muscle in the following passage:

"Teenagers are becoming mindless morons. They watch television passively. They listen passively to the latest pop tunes both on the radio and through their headphones. The follow the fashions set by peer pressure. They wear the clothes chosen by peer pressure. They smoke or take drugs as dictated by peer pressure. They have no initiative. They do no thinking of their own. They all go around in groups and feel lost without a group. They feel their parents do not understand them. They even feel that somehow society owes them a living. At the same time they feel that society is rotten and corrupt with false values. They do not know what to do, but at the same time they are not willing to listen to anyone outside their own hero group."

CHANNEL MUSCLE

If there is a channel for doing what you want to do then you can use that channel. If a channel leads to where you want to go, then you pour water into one end of the channel and it comes out where you want it. That is the basis of irrigation systems.

Channel muscle means that there already exists a *means* for doing what you want to do. Imagine that you are working for an organization that sends out 20,000 direct mail shots each week. It would be quite easy for you to arrange to put some message into each of those shots. If this channel were not available then you could look around for an organization that did this on a contract basis. That would be another channel. If, however, you set out to do it on your own then the task would be very hard.

If there is a magazine that is bought by people interested in building radio- controlled model airplanes, then you can advertise your radio control products in that magazine. You have a channel through which to reach your potential customers. If, however, you are trying to sell a left-handed screwdriver, you have a problem because there may not be a magazine that just goes to left-handed people.

The existence of a channel means that there is more *force* to what you are trying to do. That is why I call it *channel muscle.* If there is channel muscle, then your idea is more powerful than if there is no channel muscle.

In a way channel muscle is related to habit muscle. Channel muscle means that there are already standard channels in existence just as habit muscle means that there are already standard opinions (or methods) in existence. With habit muscle we have to be careful about these ready-made opinions which are used without much further thought. With channel muscle we *welcome* these existing channels because they enable us to do what we want to do. If you can use existing channels, then you are more powerful than if you have to create new channels for action.

The concept of channel muscle applies almost exclusively to active thinking. You are setting out to do something. What channels can you use?

Assessing channel muscle:

This is relatively easy. We set out what we want to do (as I shall describe in the section on 'nerves') and then we look around for *existing channels* which will allows us to do what we want to do.

1. What are we trying to do?
2. What existing channels can we use to do it?

EXERCISE

The telephone bill for your office telephones is very high. You want to find out if it is possible to reduce the expenditure. It may be that people are making too many private calls. It may be that people are spending too much time on the telephone. It may be that unauthorized people are using the telephone. What existing channels could you use for solving this problem?

MOTIVATION MUSCLE

For active thinking this is the most important muscle of them all. Nothing will ever get done unless there is motivation to do it.

Motivation muscle includes motivation, energy, will, desire, drive and want.

What is the motivation here?
How does this motivation arise?
How strong is the motivation?
Can we strengthen the motivation?

If there is no motivation then there is no *energy* in the system. Even if there are existing channels ready to be used, if there is no energy nothing will ever happen.

In my interviews with highly successful people (see the book *Tactics: The Art and Science of Success)* one of the most striking things about these people was their great energy.

There are two sorts of energy. One is the basic energy which a person can apply to anything which he or she is doing. The second type is the motivation energy which arises directly from the particular thing that is being undertaken. How motivated are you to do this particular thing?

In a well-disciplined boat crew the skipper gives the command and the crew jumps to action. It is clear that the crew members are motivated to win the race and so will obey the order. In a well-disciplined army the officer gives a command and the soldiers obey. Here we may have some doubts as to whether they are really motivated to do what is ordered. They might even resent the order. In terms of *motivation muscle,* however, their training motivates them to obey. Motivation muscle refers to the action energy, not to the particular feelings someone may have at the time. It refers to the force of action. Even a person who resents an order might carry it out with force and effectiveness.

What the masterthinker needs to do is to be conscious of motivation muscle because it is a very important factor in the effectiveness of thinking.

It also needs saying that motivation muscle applies as much to oneself as to others:
What is my motivation in doing this?
How will this motivation be sustained?

It is quite true that motivation may be derived from emotions, values and beliefs. Whatever the origin of the motivation, in motivation muscle we are directly concerned with the actual motivation (never mind the basis). That is why we need a special distinct heading for motivation muscle and why we cannot just assume that it comes under emotion muscle or value muscle or belief muscle.

Motivation muscle applies primarily to active thinking. If an action is going to take place then we need to know the motivation muscle that is going to *drive* that action. What is the energy of action?

Motivation muscle also applies to reactive thinking. What is the motivation that drives that person to write that piece or to make that speech? Here we get close to *purpose* but we can distinguish between purpose and motivation. Purpose refers to what the author is trying to do - for example to convert you to his or her point of view. Motivation refers to *why* the author is trying to do it. For example, someone may be motivated by a strong sense of injustice with regard to a particular criminal case. That person may write an article to show that the police were careless with the important evidence.

Assessing motivation muscle:

We seek to determine and to spell out the underlying motivation or energy. What is the driving force?

1. What is the motivation muscle here?
2. How does this arise?
3. How might it be altered?

The first question is the key question. We can, however, proceed to the next two questions in particular cases. For example, if we find that the acceptance of a new idea seems negative then - as part of our active thinking - we may want to know why it is negative and how we might make it positive. This goes beyond an objective definition of motivation muscle but in certain cases it is convenient to treat attempts to alter motivation at this point. For instance, if there is an obvious cause for negative motivation then we can seek to drop this from our action plan.

Examination of the motivation muscle never gets into questions of whether or not the motivation is justified. The masterthinker takes things as they are. For instance if the workers resent a new boss, the thinker takes this as the situation. It is never a matter of arguing whether they are justified in this resentment. Ways of altering this resentment may then become a *thinking objective.*

EXERCISE

Spell out the motivation muscle for each of the people involved in the following situation:

"A young woman decides to become a missionary nun. Her parents try to dissuade her because they do not think she has had a chance to see enough of life before making her choice. Her boyfriend is very upset at her decision and feels that she should not feel so guilty about the state of the world. A teacher tells her that the missionary idea is wrong and that one culture should not seek to impose its values and beliefs upon another culture. Her tutor in the missionary order tells her that the harder the decision is to make the better will the decision be in the end.

The government of the country in which she plans to work resents the colonial flavour of missionary work, but appreciates the education offered by the missionaries."

EXERCISE

What is the motivational muscle in the following situation:

You run a small food store. You want to keep it open late at night in order to give you some competitive advantage over the big supermarkets. You have to think of your family, your staff, the customers and your competitors.

Muscle: Summary

Muscle means force or power.

Muscle can refer to the force of an argument.

Muscle can refer to the power which will enable you to do what you set out to do.

Muscle is important both in reactive thinking and in active thinking. In reactive thinking we need to assess the *muscle* of what is put before us. In active thinking we need to assess the muscle of what we are trying to do.

PURPOSE

Force, power or muscle has to be exerted in some direction - towards some end. So the first thing we need to do is to examine the purpose or objective of the thinking. If it is active thinking, then we look at our own objective. If it is reactive thinking, we try to guess at the objective of the originator of the material.

In active thinking we ask:
What do we want to have at the end of our thinking?

In reactive thinking we ask:
What is the originator of the material trying to get us to feel or believe?

Note that there may be more than one objective so we should list them all.

With regard to objectives we should be aware of the following types:

Overall Objectives: What we are trying to reach in the end.

Sub-Objectives: Objectives we may have to achieve on our way to the end.

Parallel Objectives: Different objectives in parallel.

Alternative Objectives: If we do not reach that objective we can reach this other one.

Hierarchy of Objectives: Listing the objectives in order of importance.

Possible Objectives: When we are guessing at the possible objectives of others.

MUSCLE

Muscle is the force, power or energy with which we move towards the objective. I shall first list the different types of muscle and then summarize each of these in turn.

Information Muscle
Logic Muscle
Emotional Muscle
Value Muscle
Belief Muscle
Habit Muscle
Channel Muscle
Motivation Muscle

I shall now deal with each of these.

Information Muscle:

What are the facts?
What is the information base?
How hard (credible) is the information?
What is the source of the information?
What has been left out (partialism)? The two key questions become:

1. How much information do we have?
2. How hard is this information?

Hardness refers to the reliability or credibility of the information. This ranges from hard facts that we can check ourselves to the softness of rumor or hearsay.

Logic Muscle:

How do we proceed by logical steps from what we know to something new? How do we prove that our conclusion is logically based on accepted starting premises?

The two key questions become:
1. What are the starting perceptions (premises)?
2. Does this step necessarily follow?

In practice we try to identify and to spell out the 'logic lines'. This means a series of statements which we put down. We then look to see if the connection between them is necessarily so. If we can imagine an alternative explanation then the logic is probably faulty.

There are different sorts of logic from the logic of constructed systems (like mathematics) to the logic of science and language logic. There is also the logic of probability where instead of absolute certainty we use expressions like *"usually"* or *"on the whole."*

Emotional Muscle:

What are the authors' feelings and emotions on this matter (reactive thinking)? What are our feelings and emotions regarding what we are trying to do (active thinking)?

This type of muscle is particularly important in reactive thinking where the author is giving his or her feelings and trying to get us to adopt the same feelings.

The key questions are:
1. What is the author of this piece trying to do?
2. What sort of adjectives and adverbs are being used?

In order to make the emotional muscle more obvious we can go through the piece seeking to replace phrases or statements with an adjective and then examining these adjectives.

Value and Belief Muscle:

These are very often at the base of action and argument.
We seek to clarify the value system and the belief system that is being used.

The key questions are:
1. What is the value system/belief system being used here?
2. How is the thinking based on these values/beliefs?

Habit Muscle:

This refers to standard opinions, ready-made opinions, cliches, habits and patterns.

In reactive thinking we seek to pick out these standard opinions because they are often used without being examined.

In active thinking we acknowledge the difficulty of trying to change established habits and where possible we seek to use such habits for our own purposes.

The key questions are:
1. What are the standard opinions or cliches here?
2. How are they being used?

Channel Muscle:

What existing channels are there for doing what we want to do?
Are there established routes to our destination?
Can we use existing channels or must we make new ones?

This type of muscle refers particularly to active thinking. We seek to find existing channels to serve our purpose.

The key questions are:
1. What are the existing channels that serve our purpose?
2. Can we use these channels?

Motivation Muscle:

What is the motivation here?
What is the driving force?
What will provide the action energy?

In action thinking we need to assess the motivation muscle of what we are trying to do. In reactive thinking we try to assess the driving motivation of the speaker or writer of the material in front of us.

The key questions are:
1. What is the motivation or energy here?
2. What can we do about it?

We do not seek to examine whether the motivation is justified or not. We are interested in the existing motivation muscle. In certain cases we are also interested in seeking to change this.

'Muscle' is a very important part of thinking. Far too often we neglect this aspect of thinking. We believe that information and its logical connection is enough. In real life, this is never the case. In real life, the various forms of muscle listed here play a very important part. That is why the masterthinker needs to become very familiar with these types of muscle. The masterthinker must always seek to identify the type of muscle being used. This applies particularly to reactive thinking but also to active thinking.

Nerves

Bones have solidity and structure. They are tangible. They do not change.

Muscles provide force and power. They are the means of action.

Now we come to *nerves*. Nerves are for co-ordinating and organizing things. Nerves activate the muscles which then move the bones.

Nerves are *for linking things up*.

Nerves make things happen.
A nerve network is made up of tracks and connections.

In this section we shall look at *nerves* in the broadest sense of linking things up and making things happen. This section is the *organizing* aspect of thinking. In this section the active thinker will find techniques to help bring things about. The reactive thinker will find organizing frameworks to help him or her understand situations.

NETWORKS

The nerves spread out through the body to provide a network of *connections*. In an exactly similar way I shall provide a network of connections in this section. In fact I shall put forward four different networks. Each one of these four networks deals with one type of thinking. They are easy to remember because each one starts from a different edge of the paper. A piece of paper normally has four edges: top, bottom, right-hand side, left-hand side. We only have to remember the edges in order to recall the networks.

These four networks are as follows:

ACHIEVING NETWORK (starts at right-hand edge of page)
This is for finding ways and means of bringing something about.

EXPLORING NETWORK (starts at the bottom of page)
This is for exploring and expanding what we know about a subject.

ANALYSING NETWORK (starts at the top of the page)
This is concerned with analysis and classification.

ORGANIZING NETWORK (starts at left-hand side of the page)
Here things are brought together to bring about some effect.

In certain cases there may be some overlap between the different types of networks, but they are most useful if we consider them to be totally separate. We can then use each one to its maximum effect.

The diagram indicates the four directions of the four networks.

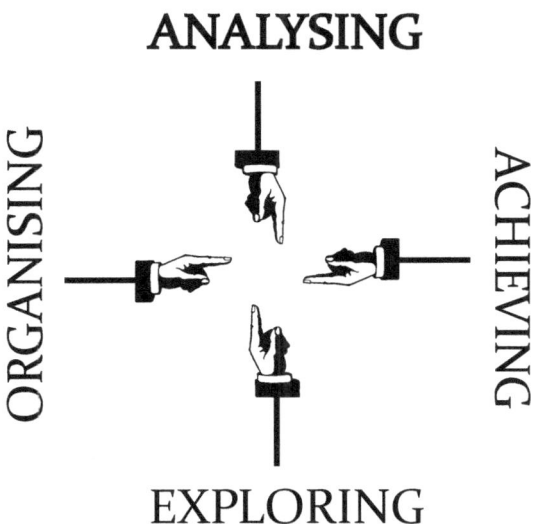

ACHIEVING NETWORK

We want to bring something about. How do we achieve it?

What are the ways and means for getting to where we want to go?

Think in terms of routes, roads, and tracks.

What are the roads which will get us there ?
We start at the right-hand side of the page and then we *work backwards* across the page.

Purpose of thinking:

At the right-hand side of the page we put down the *purpose* of our thinking. We put down where we want to get to in the end. For example, if there is the problem of a water shortage we put down "coping with a water shortage" as the purpose. As you get used to the method, you will see that sometimes you will want to define this purpose quite broadly, but at other times you may want to be very specific.

When you are using a *broad purpose,* you will find the following phrases useful:
  coping with...
  dealing with...
  doing something about...
  being successful at...
  having a way to...

Broad concepts:

Once we have down the purpose of our thinking we then look around to see what *broad concepts* will get us to that purpose. We then put these down so that each of them leads by an arrow to the purpose of the thinking. It is necessary to keep these broad concepts aligned one under the other. The procedure is shown in the diagram below.

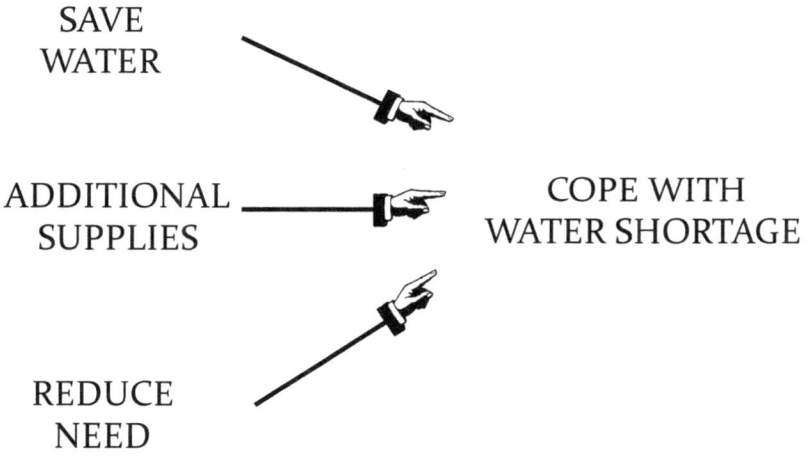

SAVE
WATER

ADDITIONAL
SUPPLIES

COPE WITH
WATER SHORTAGE

REDUCE
NEED

For example, if the purpose of thinking was "to cope with a water shortage," then the broad concept level might include the following:

  save water
  find additional supplies
  reduce need for water

Means:

We now move backwards across the page. We treat each of the broad concepts as the place we want to reach and we find alternative means for carrying out that broad concept. Each of these means feeds into that concept which will be carried out by these means. So now we get a second layer as we move backwards across the page. This is shown in the diagram.

80

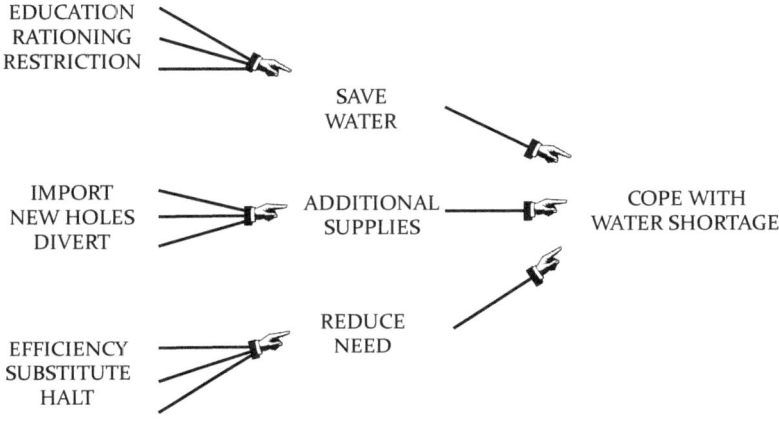

It should be said that at no point in the achievement network is there any limitation on the number of points that can be put down. You should certainly make an effort to do more than put down a single route. The effort is to find alternative routes.

With the water shortage problem, we can take each of the broad concepts in turn and find *means* to carry them out:

Save Water
The means could include: education, rationing, restriction

Find Additional Supplies
The means could include: importing water into the area, new bore holes, divert from neighbourhood supplies

Reduce Need For Water
The means could include:
making processes more efficient (for example, toilets which use one gallon to flush instead of the normal six)
using a substitute for water (for instance making paper with air instead of water)
halting water using operations.

Detail:

We now come to the detail level. Here we actually go into the detailed way in which we are going to carry out each of the means put down in the network. So we continue to move leftward across the page. Each one of the *means* on the page now becomes an achievement point. What alternative ways do we have for implementing this means? As before, we try to find as many alternatives as possible. Moving from the right-hand side of the page backwards to the left-hand side we now have four layers: purpose, broad concept, means, detail. This is shown in the diagram below. For the sake of simplicity I have just shown two alternatives in each case.

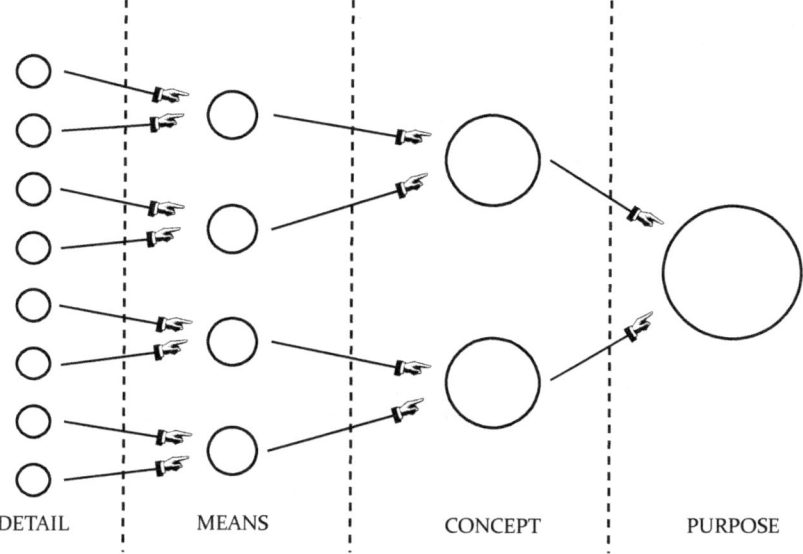

DETAIL   MEANS   CONCEPT   PURPOSE

In the case of the water shortage problem we can now explore for detailed ways of implementing the means. Some examples:

Education
This can be achieved by: media, advertising, school teaching, competitions

Restriction
This can be achieved by: lowering the pressure, turning off the water for hours at a time, making people use standpipes in the street, penalizing heavy consumption (and having spot checks)

Further detail:

There is no magic about the four layers that I have described. In some cases you may want to go further and put in another layer of detail. On the whole, however, the four layers are quite sufficient. It is enough to remember these four layers.

Fan of possibilities:

At the end we have a large number of possibilities at the left-hand side of the page. Each one of these possibilities is a way of achieving what we want to achieve. The purpose of the *achievement network* is to open up this fan of possibilities. The network helps us to do this by focusing our thinking at every moment. As we go through the network at each moment we are saying to ourselves: *How do I achieve this ?* What we are trying to achieve becomes progressively more detailed as we move backwards towards the left-side of the page.

Second draft:

When you come to try out some achievement networks you will find that it is not quite as easy as it seems. The greatest difficulty occurs with the *broad concept* layer. Most people put down detail or means at this level. It is quite hard to think in broad concept terms. When you come to look at the first draft of your network, you may find something at the broad concept level which should be pushed back to the 'means' level. For example, in the water shortage problem someone might have put "stop washing cars and clothes." This does not seem right so we ask ourselves the following question:

This is a way of doing what?

To stop washing cars and clothes is a way of "reducing the need for water." So this concept should be placed on the detail level heading into the *means* of "halting water using operations" which in turn leads into the broad concept "reducing need for water."

Note that a particular item may occur at more than one place on the network. For example, you might have put "to stop washing cars and clothes" as a detailed way of saving water - leading through a *means* of "changing habits."

The purpose of the achievement network is to open up possibilities.

Cascade effect:

If you think immediately of specific ways of achieving your objective then you will certainly get some. The purpose of the achievement network is to open up many more because of the "cascade effect." By putting in the intermediate steps, our mind is forced to think more deeply. This contrast is shown in the diagram below:

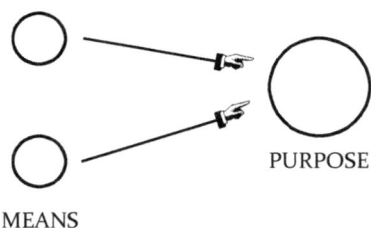

MEANS

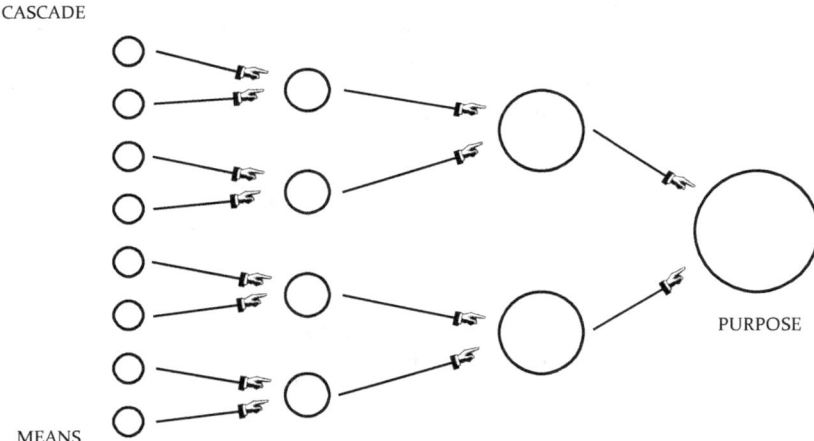

Detail to concept - and back again:

If we happen to think of a detailed way of achieving what we want to achieve, we ask ourselves the question: This is a way of doing what? That leads us up to a broader concept. Once we have this broader concept, we can look for other ways of carrying it out. This is exactly like tracing the parents of a child in order to discover the other brothers and sisters. The process is shown in the diagram.

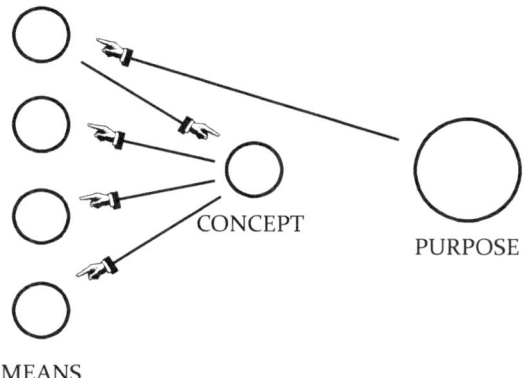

MEANS

Further alternatives

At each point in the achievement network we are asking the question:
What alternative ways do I have of achieving this? We make an effort to find
further alternatives. If we cannot find such alternatives or if we are not satisfied
with the ones we have, then we treat that as a specific thinking focus. Our
objective now becomes to find alternatives to serve exactly this process. We
can - if we wish - plug in the creative thinking procedure that I shall be dealing
with later.

EXERCISE -

*For each of the following thinking objectives, put down the broad concept layer
of an achievement network:*

> *reducing street crime*
> *stopping people smoking*
> *getting a summer job*

EXERCISE -

*The purpose of the thinking is to reduce traffic congestion in cities. The
following suggestions are made. Some of them are at broad concept level and
some are not. Pick out those that are broad concepts. For the others, answer
the following question: This suggestion is a way of doing what?
Put down the broad concepts that you find in this way.*

The suggestions are:
> *ban cars from city centres*
> *put wheel clamps on illegally parked cars*
> *improve public transport*
> *encourage car pooling*
> *replace buses with trams*
> *extend the subway system*
> *build overhead roadways*
> *stagger working hours*

85

EXERCISE -

Construct a full scale achievement network to serve the following thinking purpose:

You are running a family restaurant. A fast food restaurant opens down the road and you start to lose business. You want to find ways of attracting more business.

When you have constructed the achievement network go through it and pinpoint those areas where you feel you would like additional alternatives (where you are not satisfied with your thinking).

EXPLORING NETWORK

The exploring network starts from the bottom of the page and expands upwards.

Imagine the rising sun starting to appear over the horizon. The sun's *rays* spread upwards in a sort of fan.

The purpose of the exploring network is *to explore.* With this network we explore a subject. We expand on the subject and elaborate our thinking.

The network acts as a prompt and as a focusing aid.

The exploring network is a form of note-taking aid.

It is important to realize that in the exploring network we put down whatever comes to mind. One point suggests another. We may move from a minor detail to a very fundamental point — or the other way around. We may move from detail to detail then to a fundamental point then back to detail. This is quite unlike the achievement network where we must move from broad concept to *means* to detail.

Subject:

The subject matter is put down at the centre of the bottom of the page.

The definition of the subject matter is not so vital as it is with the other networks, because of the association nature of the exploring network. If, however, we want the exploration to stay close to the subject matter then we might have to define this much more exactly.

Expansion:

In the next layer as we move upward we put down a number of points that arise from the subject matter. There should not be more than about four of these. If you put down too many points at this level then there is no room for expansion later. So try to put down the more basic points. These form the first expansion layer.

Suppose that the subject matter was "breakfast." The start of the exploring network might look something like what is shown here:

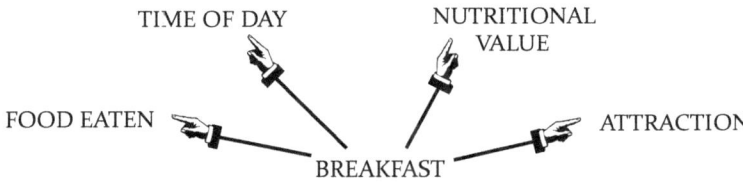

Further expansion:

The existing points define different stems for the *expansion tree.* Each stem can then expand into further branches and these in turn can expand into twigs. After the first level there is no need to try to keep things on the same level. Each point becomes a point for further expansion and exploration. So long as lines are used to show relationships (to represent the branches and twigs) different points can occur on different levels. Note that this is unlike the achievement network where the levels must be kept.

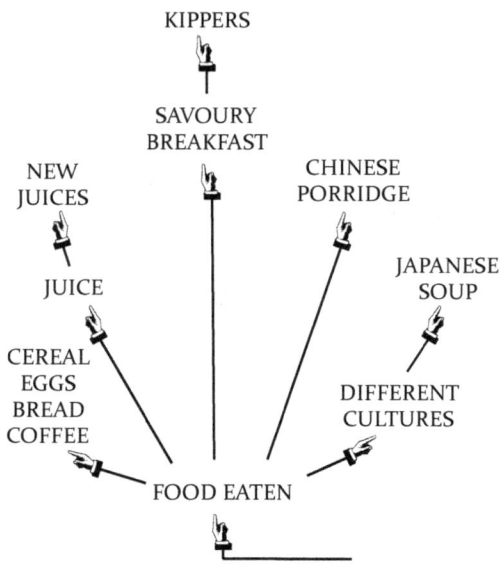

The illustration above shows how one stem of the exploration tree might develop. One thing suggests another. The tree keeps on growing upwards. Note that the concept of "savoury breakfast" grows out of the detail of "Chinese porridge." This in turn grows out of "Japanese soup" which in turn grows out of a broad concept of "different cultures."

The key idioms are: growth, expansion, elaboration and exploration. Each point that is put down becomes a potential growth point for new items. In the achievement network each point that is put down becomes an achievement point and we then figure out how to get there. In the exploration network we move outward from a point; in the achievement network we move inward towards a point.

New expansion trees:

Any point whatever on the exploration network can become a *seed* for the birth of a new tree. This seed would start off as the subject on the bottom of a fresh page. In this way there can be more space to explore particular concepts. Also small points can be explored in even greater detail. Remember that at all times the purpose is exploration and elaboration.

EXERCISE -

Construct a full exploration network for the following subject: traffic lights.

Then pick one of the points and use it as a seed to start another exploration network.

EXERCISE -

You are writing an essay on Computers and Society. Draw up an exploration network for this subject. Grow it until it contains about twenty points in all.

Although the idiom is very much that of *growth* and *growing and expansion tree,* there is a crucial difference between an exploration network and an ordinary tree. In an ordinary tree the fruit only hangs from the ends of the final twigs (or the sides). In the exploration network very important points often lie at the branch points.

To some extent we can assess the importance of any point by the weight of *foliage* which arises from that point.

How do we use the exploration network?

Very often the network is an end in itself. As we go through the exercise our mind is forced to consider a number of different points. This is the real purpose of the exercise. At other times we may want to take the output of the exercise to use in another way. One way of doing this might simply be to create major headings under each of which the detail can be described. In a more formal manner the masterthinker can move from the exploration network to the analysis/classification network. This would provide a means of putting the ideas into some order. The exploration network might also be used along with the organizing network.

The lack of tight structure in the exploration network is important because we do want to be able to put down whatever comes to mind at any moment. It is not a matter of searching for a particular concept.

ANALYSING NETWORK

This is the classic analysing network.

It is also the classic classification network.
Analysis and classification are two different things, but they make use of the same type of network. The key idiom is *division.* In analysis we divide something up into its parts. In classification we *divide* a major heading into subheadings and so on.

The analysis network starts at the top of the page - in the classic manner.

Let us look first at the analysing use of this type of network.

Subject:
The subject matter that is to be analysed comes at the top of the page - in the centre.

We do need to be quite precise with our definition of the subject matter. This is because it is difficult to analyse something vague. The subject matter can be broad (such as "running hotels") or it can be specific ("hotel restaurants").

Analysis or division:

We now attempt to divide the subject into its main components. This usually takes the form of analysis which means dividing something into its constituent elements. Sometimes the division is not a true analysis but a division of convenience. Suppose we choose to talk about the "top end", "middle piece" and "bottom end" of a walking stick. In practice, the middle piece and the bottom end are always the same piece. So it would be a division of a perceptual convenience.

Suppose that our subject was "law and order." We might analyse this into its component elements:

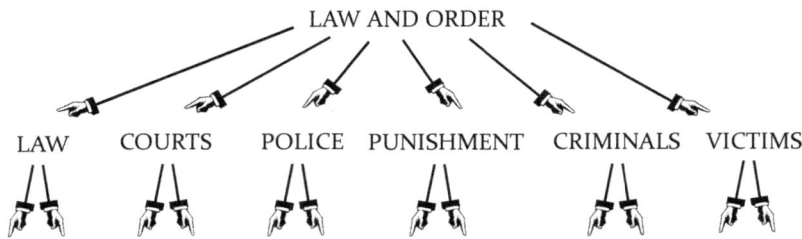

LAW AND ORDER

LAW COURTS POLICE PUNISHMENT CRIMINALS VICTIMS

Each of these major headings would then be analysed or divided up again. So each point we produce becomes a point for further division just as each point in the exploration network becomes a point for growth, and in the achievement network a point for achievement. For example, "police" could be divided into: administration, enforcement of regulations, organizing function, prevention of crime, detection of crime. "Prevention of crime" may be subdivided into: police presence, security and alarm systems, vigilant citizens, fear of detection, education, better economic conditions.

It may be noted that in this case the analysis network comes quite close to the achievement network. If we set out to analyse the "prevention of crime", we can end up listing ways of preventing crime. The point is that a *functional analysis* will seek to discover how something works. A *physical analysis* will seek to break it down into its components. For example, a physical analysis of the police would have given: personnel, equipment, buildings, finance. The type of analysis will be determined by the purpose of our thinking. If we are seeking to set up a police force, then a physical analysis would be appropriate (also if we were seeking to cut costs). If, however, we are seeking to improve the efficiency of the police force, then a functional analysis is more appropriate.

The key idiom is division and the key question is: How do I divide this up?

We can note three types of division:

1. Into the original elements that came together to give the whole.
2. Into the elements that we choose.

3. Into functional elements.

Why do we want to analyse things?

In order to understand them.

In order to know how to deal with them.

An analysis should be comprehensive. It is not just a matter of picking out some features (as it would be with finding the big bones).

If we had to analyse a vacation we might put down: timing, duration, getting there, the place, the enjoyment, the cost. We could then analyse "enjoyment" into: setting, company, activities, food, climate.

EXERCISE -

Analyse each of the following into the first level of subdivision:
school
sausage
a romance
aggression

Further division:

Each point in the first level of the division can then be divided further to give the next level and so on. An attempt should be made to keep things orderly and on defined levels (contrast with the exploration network where this does not matter). Some lines of division will become much longer than others. The items on the same level may not really be at the same level of detail. This does not matter too much. When it does seem to matter you can draw horizontal lines which define the level of detail in any way you like. Items of equivalent *size* then have to fall on the same line.

Classification use of the network:

The key idiom in classification is the grouping of things under different headings.

If we start at the top with our major heading, then the first row contains the major sub-headings. The next row contains the subheadings and so on down. For example, if we were classifying the public media, we might do it as follows:

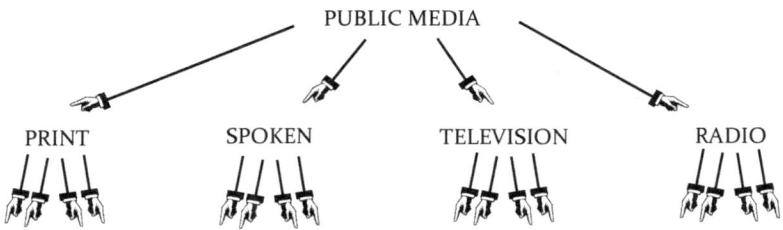

Under print we might have:

newspapers
books
magazines
leaflets

Under spoken we might have:

political speeches
church sermons
theatre

Under television we might have:

news
current affairs
documentary
drama
entertainment
soap opera

Under radio we might have:

news
current affairs
drama

You will have noted that we might have classified the types of television quite differently. We might have put:
network TV
local TV
cable TV
satellite TV
video tape

Similarly, right at the start we might have chosen to classify the types of public media as: electronic, paper, personal.

Just as we can analyse things in different ways so we can classify things in different ways. We need to choose the basis of classification and then stick to it. For example, in the classification of public media we could have chosen "audience size" as the basis of classification and might have had: millions, thousands, hundreds, tens.

The choice of the classification basis depends very much on the purpose of your thinking. What do you want to do with the classification? *In all cases,* it is worth trying out different classifications in order to see which one is the most useful. After all the sole purpose of a nerve network is usefulness.

EXERCISE -

Set out the first line of classification for each of the following subjects:
sports
airplanes
political systems
leisure activities

Working up and down:

In setting up a classification we usually find ourselves working *up and down.* This means that we think of examples and then look to see what sort of grouping they would suggest. For example, in considering leisure activities we might think of going to a concert or swimming. This might then suggest a classification of "cultural" or "exercise." We might then think of enjoying good food. This in turn might suggest one classification of "hobby" and another of "physical pleasure." This process of working up and down is exactly similar to the one we came across in the achievement network where we had to work backwards and forwards between *detail* and *means.* With classification we might ask: What group does this seem to belong to?

Working upwards from the bottom:

Although the analysing network usually works from the top down, it is occasionally necessary with the classification used to work from the bottom upwards. This happens when we have a number of different items which we are seeking to put into groups. We try things out in different groupings. When we have the simplest groups then we try to move to broader groups by combining the simpler groups. Gradually we work our way up the classification.

EXERCISE -

I shall list here a number of examples of human behaviour. See if you can create a classification for them.

saying "good morning" to an acquaintance
stealing from a shop
voting for a politician
getting drunk
smoking a cigarette
saving money in the bank
driving a car too fast
buying a new book
exchanging gossip
reading the newspaper
writing a letter of complaint
climbing a high mountain
quarrelling with your family
helping a blind person cross the road
throwing an empty beer can into the street
telling a lie

Why do we bother to classify things? In order to detect similarities and differences. If we know that something is a member of a certain group, then we expect to find all the characteristics of that group. This is the purpose behind botanical and medical classifications. At other times it is for a sense of order and tidiness.

In the exploration network you might have turned up a number of points. You could then use the classification network to put those points into some sort of order so that you could write a report or an essay. In such a piece of writing the major headings would describe the sections and then subheadings and sub-subheadings would form the paragraphs.

EXERCISE -

Set up a classification network for the following subject:

clothes.

Write a short essay using the classification as the basis for this.

ORGANISING NETWORK

This could also be called 'project network'.

The organizing network is concerned with putting things together to bring something about. That is what happens with projects. In an office building development project, the developer has to put together the land, the financing, the potential client, and the construction company. Then the project can get under way.

In many constructive situations we find that if we put A together with B then we have C (A+B=C). In cooking we put the ingredients together, then we apply heat—and we end up with a meal. This general principle applies throughout to the organizing network. Gunpowder + ignition = explosion. Obviously we want an explosion in the barrel of a gun, in fireworks or in a blasting charge - but not in the factory or the store. So we need to control or *organise* so things happen at the right time.

In the organising network, we start at the left-hand side of the page.

We start with listing the ingredients that we have or that we are going to need. Usually we list the ingredients that we know we are going to use in the project. For the start of the development project, we might have listed: land, financing, tenant, construction company.

Occasionally, with the organising network we may put down things we have in order to see what we can do with them. This is an exploratory type of organisation. On the whole, the organizing network is concerned with bringing about a known objective from known ingredients. The purpose of the network is to organize things to create the desired end result.

List of ingredients:

We put down the list of things that we need. This also includes the list of things that have to be done. For example, after the development project is under way, the construction company will need to organize what it is going to do. The list of ingredients might look something like this:

dig foundations
delivery of steel
construction of steel frame
concrete formwork
concrete
fit glass panels
put in doors and windows
plaster walls
electrical supplies
plumbing
data networks
carpets
furnishings
furniture

All these are elements or ingredients that will be needed in moving from a bare piece of land to a completed office building.

Timing:

A key element in organising things is *timing*. In the example of the gunpowder, I indicated that you only wanted the gunpowder to explode at the right time. So timing is always part of our control or management of a situation.

In the construction project we cannot put in the carpets until the flooring is in place. We cannot put in doors and windows until there are walls. We cannot pour the concrete until the formwork is in place. We cannot construct the steel frame until the steel has been delivered. We cannot begin to construct the steel frame until the foundations have been dug.

If A+B=C and C+D=K, then it is obvious that we cannot add C to D until we have C. And we will not have C until we have added A to B. So there is an organizing sequence that we have to observe.

We can now look again at part of the construction project:

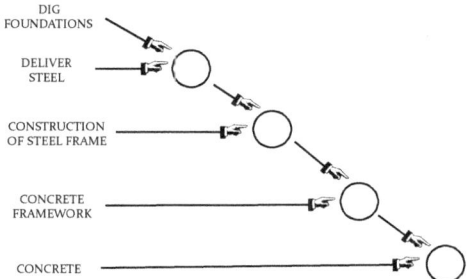

It is clear that we cannot have the steel delivered until we have dug the foundations because this would make it difficult to dig the foundations. So the first thing is to dig the foundations. When that is done we *add* the delivery of steel. Then we add the steel construction. Now that we have the steel frame we start the concrete formwork. Then we *add* the concrete.

These *additions* or coming together processes are shown by lines on the organising network. When two things come together we have a node which indicates either that something is completed or that something has been brought about. For example we need a node to indicate that the digging of the foundations is completed. Completed foundations plus delivered steel is another node (in fact we might only deliver the steel as we were using it).

Time lines:

We need to choose our order, our sequence, and our timing. But sometimes we have to wait for things to happen. For example, concrete requires some time to set. We cannot hurry this along. Also digging the foundations requires some time. In order to see when things can happen we need to put on the organising network some indication of real time. Note that this does not apply to all organising networks.

We use a vertical line to indicate a certain time. For example, a vertical line could represent seven days and another one ten days and so on. All the things that happen exactly at that time are shown on the line. Things that happen before or after are shown before or after that line. This process is shown with the construction example:

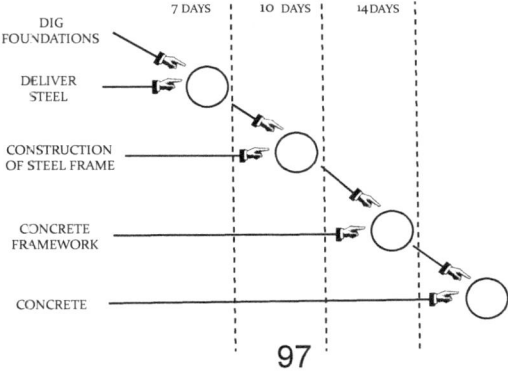

97

Everything does not have to follow along one straight line. For example, a big steel sculpture might be part of the building. The sculptor may start work on that even before the foundations are dug. He works on it in parallel - as a sort of *mini-project*. The sculpture must however, be ready to be lifted into place while the construction cranes are still on site. So it does have to come into the stream of things at the right moment. Similarly pre-set concrete panels can be made elsewhere and then fitted into place at the right moment. The more things that can happen in parallel the quicker the process will be.

Modification:

Once you have set out the organizing network you can modify and improve it. One of the main purposes of all four networks is to make it possible for the thinker to see his or her thinking and then to improve this. We can modify the organizing network by changing the issues, the sequence, the timing, the words we use, etc. We may simply want to modify the order in which we list the ingredients so as to give a neater network. For instance in the construction example, plumbing and electrical work have to come before plastering the walls so these items could be higher up the list - to avoid crossed lines in the network.

An author and her literary agent are discussing her next book. They are deciding the plan of action to follow. Should she write the book she wants and then look around for a suitable publisher? Or should she just put down a synopsis and find an interested publisher and then proceed from that basis? The ingredients are as follows:

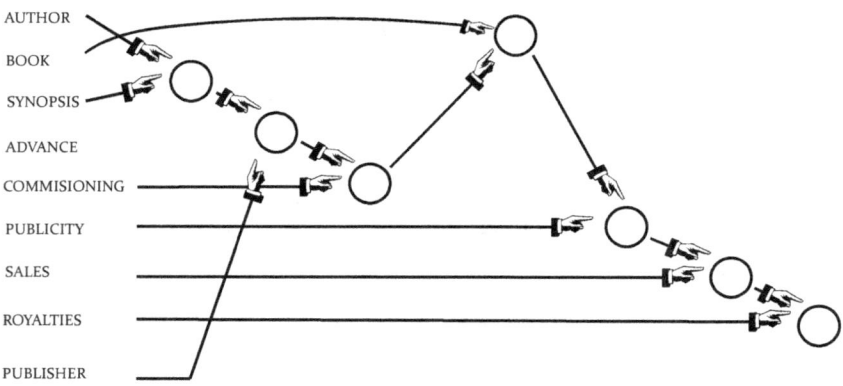

The preceding network shows one particular way of organizing the situation. A different way is shown below. This time we need to introduce—as another ingredient - the concept of *auction* in which the completed book is offered to the highest bidder.

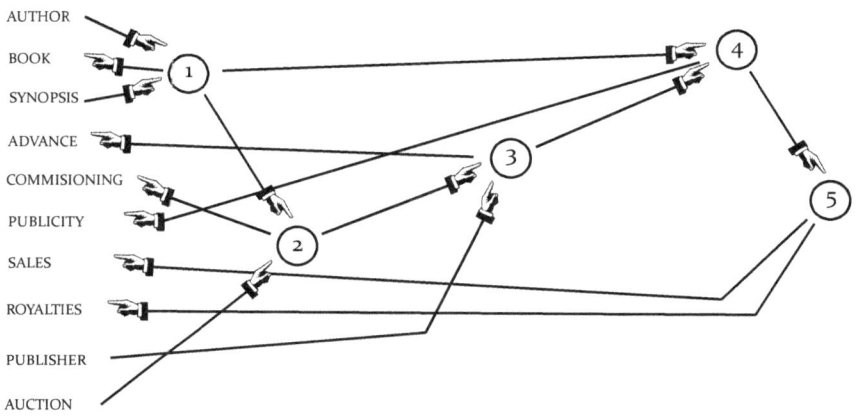

Note that in this example "sales" and "royalties" are not actual inputs. The author and publisher cannot force anyone to buy the book. So sales and royalties are "outputs." They are things that happen if all goes according to plan. Nevertheless we can include them in the organizing network because they *occur* at this point. If you wish you can show an arrow pointing towards the left-hand margin of the paper to indicate "output."

Labelling the network:

As with all the other networks you can use words at junction points on the network itself - if there is room. Otherwise you can use a number as a code indicator and then list the labels elsewhere under their numbers. This can be particularly important in the organizing network because when two things are brought together, there may be something new which needs a descriptive label. In the author example, if the author and publisher had a discussion the result might be that the publisher would commission a book. We can show this in one of two ways:

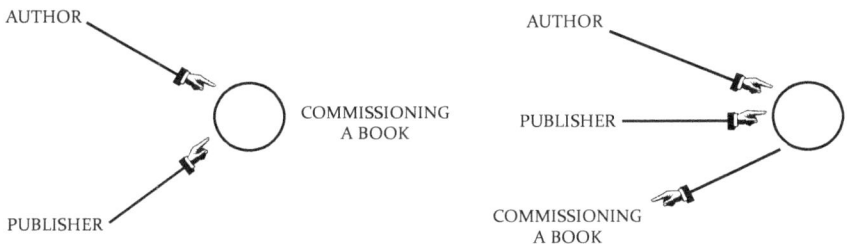

99

The first example is perhaps easier to follow, if there is enough space. The second example has the advantage that you can list inputs and desired outputs on the same list - but there can be a confusion of lines.

EXERCISE -

You want to install new plumbing in the bathroom of your apartment. This may take some days work. Make a simple organizing network showing how you would organize the matter (including your daily life).

EXERCISE -

A new strain of polio virus has emerged and a few cases have been reported. There is a need to carry out a massive immunization campaign, especially on school children. How would you organize this? Draw an organizing network showing the steps.

EXERCISE -

You are planning to make your fortune in real estate. Draw an organizing network showing the steps that you would take (including training).

Build-up network:

As I mentioned earlier, the organizing network can occasionally be used as a *build-up* network. This means that we start out with the ingredients and then *try to see* what can be done with them. This is in contrast to the project network where we do know exactly what we are trying to do.

For example, a person who has recently lost his job is trying to figure out what to do. He lists as his ingredients:

10 years experience in the oil industry
no family
computing as a hobby
knowledge of Arabic
Greek father

Ten years experience in the oil industry could come together with knowledge of Arabic to suggest a job in the Middle East. No family and a Greek father (possibility of Greek passport) suggest a freedom to work in most countries. Computing as a hobby suggests specializing in data processing for the oil industry. So the plan might be to learn more about computers, specialize in DP for the oil industry. Take a job in the Middle East in this type of work. Return to the U.S.A. as an expert in this field.

The organizing network can also be used on the output of the exploring network. The exploring network will provide a number of items. These could form the ingredient list. We could then look to see how these came together to give a result. This could form the basis of an essay or a report. I have mentioned earlier that the classification (grouping) network can also be used in this way. The difference is that the classification network will give an order and tidiness through providing headings. The organizing network is more likely to give a final result.

The key point in using the build-up network is to see what happens when two things come together: what results, what do they produce, what happens?

You have the following ingredients, what can you make of them?

a vegetable garden
a refrigerator
a van
two dozen chairs

The vegetable garden and the chairs suggest a vegetarian restaurant. The van then suggests a vegetarian delivery service. The final idea might be the delivery of complete vegetarian meals to other restaurants for those diners who want vegetarian meals. Note that in the end the chairs and direct vegetarian restaurant idea have dropped out.

EXERCISE -

You have the following list of ingredients, what could you do with them?

lots of old clothes, a skill in carpentry, a friend who is a dentist, a knowledge of airline companies, training as an actor, a house in a country town

(note that if you need any added 'crucial ingredients ' you could always acquire these).

EXERCISE -

You are writing an essay on the subject of "sleep" and your exploration network has given you the following points. What use can you make of them?

different people need different amounts of sleep
what is the right amount of sleep
insomnia is a big problem for some
sleeping pills
coffee is a stimulant that keeps some people awake
the best time for going to bed
reading in bed helps some people sleep
sleep might be a habit
do we feel better if we sleep more
there is dream sleep and non-dream sleep
dreams may be useful in sorting out emotional problems

Nerves:
Summary

Bones indicate the basic elements.
Muscle indicates power or force.
Nerves are for connecting things up.

The human body has a nerve network and so for the "nerves" approach we use connecting networks. There are four types of networks that we are going to use. I shall list them all first and then summarize each in turn.

ACHIEVING NETWORK

How we get there. How we achieve something.

EXPLORING NETWORK

Exploring what we know about a subject. Growing an expansion tree.

ANALYSING NETWORK

For divisions and sub-divisions as used in analysis or classification.

ORGANISING NETWORK

For bringing things together to bring about some result.
Each of the networks starts at a different edge of the page as suggested in the diagram below.

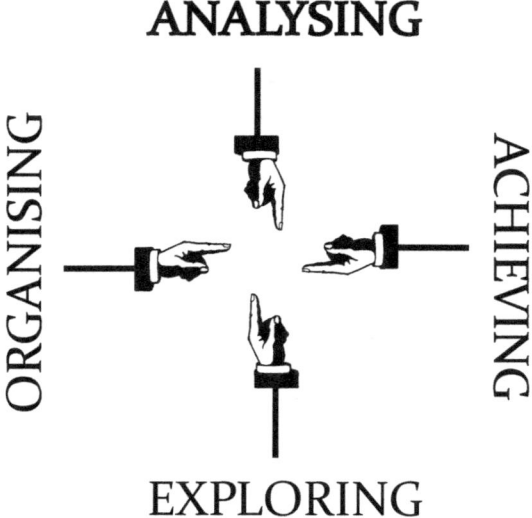

ACHIEVING NETWORK

How we bring something about.
The routes or roads for getting somewhere.
The alternative ways of bringing something about.

We start at the right hand edge of the page and put down the purpose of our thinking.

We now work *backwards*
What *broad concepts* will lead us to that purpose?

We now take each broad concept as the point we wish to reach.
What different *means* will take us to this broad concept?

We now take each of the *means* as the point we wish to reach.
What *detail* (way or method) will take us to this means?

So each point we put down becomes the *achievement point* and we think how we might reach that point. There is an emphasis on alternatives. What *different* ways of reaching this alternative can we find?

We often work from detail to concept and then back again. If a detail type of method comes to mind we ask: This is a way of doing what? That leads us to a concept and then we look for other detail methods.

EXPLORING NETWORK

What do we know or think about this subject?
A sort of expanding note-taking that stimulates us to put down ideas.

We start at the bottom of the page and put down the subject of our thinking.

At the next level above we put down some major features that come to mind. These form the *stems* of the tree we are about to grow.

We now grow an *expansion tree.* From each of the stem points we grow new points. Any connection will do. It may be function or association. There is no longer any need to keep to defined levels. The points are connected up by lines - thus giving the *tree* which grows upwards.

Any point in the exploring network can be taken out and can become the subject for a new exploring network or another sheet of paper.

The main idiom is that each point we put down can be expanded into other points.

The output of the exploring network can be fed into either an organising network or an analysing network used in the classification mode (grouping).

ANALYSING NETWORK

This is concerned with division and sub-division.
The same network can be used for analysis or classification.
How do we divide this up?
What are the components here?
What comes under this heading?

We start at the top of the page and put down the subject we are considering by the major heading.

We now analyse or divide the subject into its main components. This forms the first line of the division.

Then we divide each division into sub-divisions. This forms the next line. We proceed in this way. The network spreads as it descends the page.

We can recognize three types of divisions or analysis:

1. Into the original parts that came together to give a whole.
2. Into elements that we choose.
3. Into functional elements.

The choice of the type of analysis depends on the purpose of our thinking.

The network is used in the same way for classification. Instead of dividing things up into components we seek the members of the *group* indicated by the heading. What comes under this heading?

A classification can be done on different basis. It is necessary to define the basis of the classification before commencing.

We can occasionally use the classification method in the reverse order. We can start at the *bottom* and then see how we can group things together. Then we see how we can group these groups - and so on. In this way we work upwards from the bottom of the page towards the top.

The main idiom of the analysing network is to see how each point can be divided into other points.

ORGANISING NETWORK

We put things together to bring things about.
How and when do we put these things together?
At what point can we start doing this?
The organizing network is for constructing things.
The organizing network is used for projects.

We start at the left-hand side of the page and we put down a list of ingredients.

The basic idiom of the organizing network is: A + B = C.
An ingredient (A) comes together with an ingredient (B) and the result is something else (C).

Sometimes one thing cannot happen until another thing has happened so there has to be a control of sequence. You must make the coffee before you can drink it. On other occasions, a process takes some time and we may have to wait until that is complete until we proceed. Boiling water for the coffee takes time.

A timeline is a vertical line which indicates some time in the future. If something happens before that time, it is placed before that line. If it happens after that time, it is placed after that line. Anything that happens at that time goes on the line itself. It is not necessary to use timelines with every organising network.

When things come together to give a result we can label that *outcome* at the junction point on the network itself. Alternatively we can put the *outcomes* down in the ingredient list and then use an arrow from the junction to the item to indicate that it is an outcome and not an input.

The organising network can also be used *to see what we can make* out of a number of ingredients. In this case we start off with the ingredients and then see what happens when we combine them in different ways. This method can be used for organising the output produced by an exploring network.

In general organising networks have a known and defined objective. The purpose is to see how we can organise what we have to produce that objective.

GENERAL COMMENT

There are times when the networks may seem to be doing the same thing. For example an analysing network using functional analysis may be similar to an achieving network. The basic idiom of each network is, however, quite distinct and you will get most value out of each network if you treat them as such. Be very clear in your mind as to the idiom and purpose of each type of network.

Do you want to achieve something?
Do you want to explore something?
Do you want to analyse something?
Do you want to organise something?

Fat

Have you seen a really gaunt face without any fat on it? The bones seem to be almost coming through the skin. It is the fat that provides the roundness and attractiveness of the human face - and the human body too.

On the other hand there are people who seem obviously too fat. That is to say they are much fatter than most other people. Being fat is a style and is attractive in its own way. Historically there have been many cultures and many famous painters who have put a high value on being fat. From a medical point of view being excessively fat is something of a health risk. When a person is very fat it is obvious that the bones are well hidden by the fat.

In the BFT system we have looked at bones, muscles, and nerves and now we come to look at *fat*.

We can contrast fat with bones. The bones are the essential structural elements. They are the basic elements. Without the bones there is no form and structure. In contrast *fat* refers to the detail, the padding, the elaboration. None of this fat is strictly necessary. There is also no limit to the amount of fat there might be. If something is not essential then it may be *fat*.

We can contrast fat with muscle. *Muscle* gives force and power to the thinking. Fat does not give force. Fat only gives bulk. A written piece may be bulky because of all the fat - but this does not add to the force of the argument. Sometimes it does seem as if the writer or speaker believes that more and more detail add to the importance of the thinking. This is never the case. If the force of the argument is weak, then further details do not make it stronger. If the force of the argument is strong, then further detail may only blur the force of the argument.

The assessment of *fat* applies particularly to reactive thinking. You are reading a letter, a book or a report and you attempt to pick out the bones, muscle and fat. You may find that at the end you have a few strong bones and a great deal of fat. You may be listening to a political speech and as you listen you make a mental note of the muscle of the argument. Then you note all the fat that is really unnecessary to the argument, but is being used to persuade the audience.

The idea of *fat* also applies to active thinking. A group of people are sitting around a table figuring out how to work on some project. In the discussion there is a great deal of talk that would be best described as *fat*. This extra talk does not really add much. It provides neither the bones of what must be done nor the muscle force of why something will work.

These things we are discussing now are just *fat*. They are detail. They do not add to the basic structure (bones) of what we need to do. Nor do they add to the force of our plan (muscle). Let's get down to essentials!

The masterthinker needs to have a strong sense of *fat*. That is to say a strong sense of the difference between essentials and non-essentials. This does not mean that the masterthinker has to stop at each moment to say "that is fat." At the back of the masterthinker's mind, however, there is this warning light that flashes on and indicates *FAT* whenever the thinker comes across unnecessary material.

PICKING OUT THE FAT

You may suppose that if you have already picked out the bones and the muscle then whatever else is left is the fat. You would be right. In practice it is worth making the special effort to pick out the fat directly because this sets up thinking habits that the thinker can then use in his or her own thinking.
It is important that the thinker is able to say: "That is fat."

EXERCISE -

In the following passage pick out the fat.
"This is the way you get to the copy shop. When you get out of the door and on to the street, you turn right. You stay on the same side of the road. You will pass the hardware store, then there is a shop that sells office equipment such as typewriters, copiers, and small business computers. I think they have models of the new IBM PC - you know the one that allows you to do clever things with statistics. They may not have received it yet. I read about it only last week. The next place you come to is a shop that sells clothes. I do not know who their customers are. The clothes always seem of rather poor quality and at a very high price. They had an awful pink dress in the window yesterday. I suppose someone must buy the clothes otherwise they would go out of business. Perhaps it is just as well that people have different tastes otherwise we should all look alike."

"Next comes a shop that sells fruit and vegetables. It could be run by Koreans. I do not know if it is, but someone once told me that in New York city the Koreans have taken over all the sales of fruits and vegetables. I suppose it is because they are more efficient and no one else could make it pay. I have not actually seen any Koreans there - but then I do not do my shopping there. I usually shop on weekends at that great big supermarket at the edge of town. Have you ever been there? The parking is so much easier than shopping in town. If you go there at one o'clock on Saturday, it is usually quite empty - I suppose everyone is having their lunch. Anyway, after this vegetable store - you cannot miss it because all the vegetables and fruit are displayed on the sidewalk - comes a jeweller. It is a small shop with lots of rings in the window.

"I cannot imagine who buys all these rings. I can see that people buy rings when they are getting married or something like that. But that cannot be enough business to keep them going. I have heard that in certain parts of Europe all the married men wear rings so that women can tell that they are married. Perhaps their wives insist on that. What do you think of that idea?"

"So, there is this little jeweller with the rings in the window. Then there is this great big yellow sign which says 'Copy Shop'. You cannot really miss it. In fact, you can see it as soon as you step out into the street and look right. Now that is where you get the copies done."

Now that particular exercise is something of an exaggeration which is intended to show that the *fat* may sometimes be clearly visible. At other times it may be much more difficult to pick out.

In order to pick out the fat we must have a very clear idea of the purpose of the thinking (see the section on 'muscle'). What may be fat in one context may not be fat in another.

EXERCISE -

Pick out the fat in the following piece:
"He came into the shop at about noon. I think it was about noon but I cannot be absolutely sure. My watch has not been working well lately and I took it last week to Joe's - you know that small shop down by the bus station - to get it repaired. The trouble with watches nowadays is that when they are broken no one wants to repair them. In fact it is almost cheaper to get a new one. I think this repair is going to cost me about $30 and I could buy one of those small digital watches for about $20. They are made in Hong Kong or something. But I do not like digital watches. I like the old-fashioned kind with a face and hands. You know where you are then. I don't go for modern things just because they are new. Some of them are just gimmicks. But I suppose they are good business. People do buy them. My friend Tom has bought three digital watches in the last year. Each one of them has some new gimmick. One of them tells the time in eight different countries. What use is that unless you are going to telephone people in all those countries?

"Anyway I think it was about noon because Mrs. Silvio had just left. She always comes in about mid-day. She does not usually buy anything; she just wants to chat. She wants someone to listen to her tales about her husband. She thinks he is a great womanizer with girlfriends all over the place. She is always telling me about her latest suspicion. I have met her husband and he is very quiet and timid and completely bullied by her. I would be most surprised if he has ever looked at another woman. Perhaps she likes to think that because it makes him more of a man than he seems to be."

"Well, she had come in and she had that sweet little girl of hers. The girl was wearing a nice little blue dress with yellow flowers around the bottom. I remember this because I have a good memory for faces and what people are wearing. I suppose it is from the days when I was in the garment business."

"Well Mrs. Silvio had just left and I was considering whether to go next door to get myself a hamburger for lunch. I can easily close the shop for twenty minutes or so. I just put a notice in the window which says "Back in 15 Minutes". I have found that it is better than giving the time you expect to be back. If you give the exact time and you are later than you can find some very angry customer waiting for you and accusing you of being late. It is my shop why shouldn't I come and go as I like. Anyway if you just put '15 minutes' then they do not know when you put that sign up. So it works much better."

"I always try to get my hamburger around noon because if I leave it any later the place fills up with all the office workers from around here. There are many of them since the building of that huge new insurance building on the corner."

"So I was just thinking of going out when this young man walks in. Now he walked in quite casually. He was wearing white sneakers with light blue laces. They were old and scuffed. I do not know the name of the make, but if you showed me some makes I am sure I would recognize them. He had on jeans. Now the jeans looked quite new. In fact they still had a bit of a crease in them. He was wearing a sort of ski type jacket, bright red in colour and probably made of nylon. That was also quite new. The shirt was a plaid shirt."

"He was a fresh-faced young man. Aged about twenty-two. I am very bad at ages. Not so long ago I met a woman and her daughter and got them confused. My wife tells that story on every possible occasion. I suppose the mother was very flattered. I am sure the daughter was not. But certain people have faces like that. You cannot tell their ages. My uncle Sam looked about forty when he was nearly sixty."

"He had on a little moustache. It seemed very neat and it was not quite the same color as his hair. I suppose that can happen. I once knew a man who had black hair and a red moustache. It looked most strange. I am sure everyone thought he dyed it. He told me it was quite natural and that his doctor has told him that there were many people like that."

"So he walked straight up to me and without saying anything more he pulled out this gun and demanded two hundred dollars. I gave it to him. What choice did I have?"

Because of the crime, some of the detail in this passage is very important. Such detail might have been fat in another passage, but it is *muscle* in this one (information type of muscle). Even so there is still a great deal of fat in the passage. That is to say detail and elaboration that have no relevance to the crime. It may be said that some of this extra detail (like the colour of the little girl's dress) is important in order to throw light on the reliability of the witness. Was he really good at noticing things?

NOTING THE CONTEXT

In assessing *fat,* it is most important to take note of the context. *As I have indicated what is fat in one situation might not be fat in another.* We need to ask how relevant the fat is to the purpose of the thinking. In a discussion about some major project one of those taking part may go into details that would be essential at a later point in the discussion, but at an early stage must be seen as fat.

EXERCISE -

Pick out the fat from the following discussion:
"The purpose of this meeting is to decide whether to locate our new plant in Minnesota. "

"I had an aunt who lived in Minnesota - she told me that it got awfully cold in the winter. Temperatures of thirty or forty below zero at times. That is very cold. I do not know if I could take that."

"There is a lot of high tech development going on up there. I am told the work force is skilled and hardworking. "

"Many of the people come from German or Swedish backgrounds, don't they? That should make them hardworking."

"I have heard the schools and colleges are very good."

"What about transportation? It is a bit out of the centre isn't it?"

That is true but then the West coast is as far as it can possibly be from the East coast and that does not seem to matter. In high tech the cost of transport is not so important. "

"Are there any tax advantages?"

"1 have the impression that they have a very serious view of business up there. It is the place that produced Hubert Humphrey. "

"1 thought he was a liberal - wanting to spend all the taxpayers money on welfare benefits and that sort of thing. Give me Reagan every time."

"That's not true about liberals. They believe that for society to work all of society must be in good shape."

"If welfare payments are too high why should anyone want to work. I am told that is what has happened in Europe. We do not want that to happen here."

"How many people would we want to move to Minnesota? Would they be willing to go? Would you be willing to go?"

"The HQ will remain here in New Jersey."

"What is the air service like between Newark and the Twin Cities. I do not like the idea of having to change planes to get there? How many flights a day are there?"

What are the arguments in favour of the move to Minnesota? What is the muscle *of this argument ?*

There are three key questions which can be asked when we are examining something for the *fat content.*

1. Is it necessary?
2. Is it relevant?
3. Is it important?

Something may be relevant but not strictly necessary. Something may be relevant, but not important. The crucial test is simple: *What would happen if we dropped this out?*

EXERCISE -

This is a reverse type of exercise.
1 want the thinker to put fat into a piece. As an exercise try to put as much fat as possible into the passage. Write a passage (about twenty lines) in which you describe how a fire in the kitchen of a neighbour's house was put out.

BEAUTY AND FAT

It is obvious that when we are writing factual material that we should keep the fat down to the minimum.

The function of fat in the human body is to add beauty. What happens when we are writing material as an art form?

"We went to the edge of the cliff. The sun set. We went home."

As a description of a sunset that is very dull. The whole purpose of art is to instil an actual experience and to go beyond this to involve human feeling and emotion. In order to do this we have to go beyond a simple factual reporting of what has happened. Descriptions of sunsets in literature describe the sun's changing hues and feelings of peace, serenity, and universality that accompany viewing of the sunset.

I would not want to give the impression that removing the fat from our thinking means removing the beauty from our work.

In fact there is no real difficulty because I have made clear that an assessment of fat content is always related to the purpose of the thinking (or writing). If that purpose is art or beauty, then any material which adds to this is - by definition - not fat.

EXERCISE -

Pick out the fat in the following description of a sunset.

"We went to the edge of the cliff beyond the simple and powerful stones of the megalithic temple at Hagar Qim on the island of Malta. Five thousand years before people had stood in that temple and also watched the sunset. There is controversy over the actual dating of the stone age temples. Some claim that the temples actually go back to 5,000 BC. The red globe of the sun was alighting gently on the horizon and the colour organ of the sky was playing the last melodies of grays and pinks. The sharp silhouette of the tiny rock islands of Filfla stood like a sentinel to the resting place of the sun. This island had been used by the British military forces as a firing range for bombs and shells. Many unexploded bombs and shell still remained on the island. In fact there was an on-going dispute between the government of Malta and the British government with regard to clearing up the mess. The government of Malta claimed that it was the responsibility of the British government since they had created the mess."

"The glow of the setting sun coloured red the huge stones of the old temple. It was the red of warmth rather than of blood. There was a feeling of universality as if the moment of sunset linked mankind over the ages. The people who had built that temple had lived thousands of years ago and yet at this moment they also seemed present at the celebration of the cycle of days and the cycle of life. The air temperature was about sixty-two degrees (Fahrenheit) and the wind was quite light - about four knots and coming from the south. Ellen was taking picture after picture, but seemed to have a great deal of difficulty deciding how to use her automatic Canon camera. The trouble with automatic cameras is that they are set for average conditions and sunsets are not average conditions. There seems to a time when technology is actually a disadvantage rather than an advantage."

"Suddenly the sun was gone and the air seemed to get colder as it signalled that the ceremony was over - but would be held again and again for thousands of years to come. And the stones of the temple would be the guardians of that ceremony as they always have been."

In this particular example the *fat* is actually the factual material that interferes with the mood or feeling of the piece.

It should be said that even when the purpose of the piece is indeed beauty or art, there can still be a lot of fat. One of the biggest problems that aspiring writers have is to know what to leave out. The excessive use of adjectives and gushing purple passages is a major fault of descriptive writing. These are certainly *fat*. The test is the same as before: What does this contribute? The idea that more must be better does not apply to art.

EXERCISE

The following is a purple passage. Trim it down by removing some of the fat.

"It was a gorgeous, marvellous and exciting spring day. The world seemed to be just coming alive in all manner of ways. The blossom buds like a snow of fertility were settled on the trees. The birds in an abandonment of sheer exuberance were swooping and climbing as they danced their aerial celebration of spring. The awful dullness and grey boredom of winter seemed like a country that was slipping away as the passengers at the rail of a cruise ship watched their last visited country disappear over the horizon. The air was as sparkling and clear as a fizzing glass of Perrier water. Everything seemed brand new. Everything seemed full of promise."

SENSE OF FAT

When it comes to picking out the bones of some thinking then it is important that this be done in a clear and defined manner. It is very important that the masterthinker gets this right.

This is just as important when it comes to assessing the muscle of the thinking. If we cannot assess the muscle of the thinking then we cannot tell how valuable it is or whether it is going to work.

When it comes to assessing the fat content of our thinking - or the thinking of others - the general 'sense' of fat is even more important. We need to have clearly in our minds a sense of what is irrelevant and unnecessary as we think about anything. We need to have this *sense* of fat clearly in our minds when we react to the thinking of others.

The masterthinker's skill at this point is not just concerned with picking out the *fat,* but with this general sense of reducing the fat. The concept is that of slimming and staying slim. Thinking should be slim and trim.

Fat: Summary

Fat is additional material.

Fat is added to the bare bones of the material.

Fat is elaboration and detail.

There may be a small amount of fat or the fat may be excessive.
The bones are the basic elements of the situation. The muscle is the force of power of the argument. The fat is the additional material.

Fat is padding. It is used by the thinker to pad out the more important material.

Assessing the *fat content* applies both to reactive and to active thinking.
With reactive thinking we try to pick out the fat in what we are reading or hearing. In active thinking we assess material for relevance to what is intended.

CONTEXT AND PURPOSE

In order to make a proper assessment of *fat content* we need to have a very clear awareness of the purpose of the thinking and the context.

For example, the discussion of certain details may be relevant to a particular subject - but at the proper moment. If outside that moment the details are irrelevant, they are fat.

If the context or purpose of a piece of writing is beauty, then the assessment of fat must be related to that purpose. Material which would be fat in another context is not fat when the purpose is beauty (art). Conversely material which would not be fat elsewhere (facts, figures) might become fat when the purpose is beauty.

There are times when detail is important. For example, in a criminal investigation or in negotiating an agreement, the detail may be vital. In such cases we would be at a disadvantage if we did not pay a great deal of attention to detail. There are other times when the detail is clearly *fat*.

So a strong sense of the purpose or context of the piece is essential.

SENSE OF FAT

It is important that the masterthinker has a strong *sense of fat*. This is quite different from the actual ability to pick out the fat. It is a background sense of fat which operates the whole time someone is thinking: What is relevant here and what is irrelevant?

120

Effective thinking should be slim and trim. This can come about if every masterthinker has a strong sense of fat. People who want to be slim watch their diets and are conscious of their figures. In a similar way the masterthinker must be always aware of the danger of fat in his or her thinking.

This sense of fat applies both to active and reactive thinking.

RELEVANCE

This is, of course, the key point about *fat*.

The three questions are:

1. Is it necessary?
2. Is it relevant?
3. Is it important?

All three of these questions need to be asked on any particular occasion. All three of these questions need to be present in the mind of the thinker. If something is not relevant, it is fat. If something is not necessary, it is fat. If something is not important, it may not be fat but it might be. There are often things which are not important but which are worth noting.

SOME FAT

I am not suggesting that the masterthinker should try to remove all fat on every possible occasion. This would be a bit dull and a bit stark. Life would not be very enjoyable if we all had gaunt faces and bodies consisting of skin wrapped bones. So the amount of fat that is tolerable depends on the context and purpose. In some cases we may strive to remove all fat (reports). In other cases we may want to keep some of the fat (essays).

The important thing is that we should be aware of the *fat* even if we then decide to keep some of it.

In my experience I have found that it is a characteristic of all good thinkers that they have a very strong sense of *fat*. That is why it is essential that any masterthinker also has a strong sense of fat.

In some situations, there may be argument as to whether something is, or is not, fat. Often case can be made either way. In such instances it is best to accept the alternative view. Making a decision about whether something is or is not fat, is much less important than having a general sense of *fat* and the ability to assess *fat content*.

Skin

It is sometimes said that beauty is only skin deep. It is difficult to be beautiful if the skin is poor. The human face and the human body is enclosed in skin.

When we look at someone we look at the skin. To be sure the bones, fat and muscle beneath the skin are what give it shape. Indeed there are faces where the true beauty is given by the bone structure. Nevertheless the *skin* is the outer wrapping.

In the BFT method the skin stands for the appearance or presentation. The *skin* is indeed the wrapping. The skin is the wrapping in which our thinking is enclosed in order that it may be presented to others or to ourselves.

I have often come across very good thinking that is so poorly presented that no one is able to appreciate the excellence of that thinking.

In my considerable experience in the field of thinking I would say that presentation is very important. Anyone who believes that presentation is superfluous and that the quality of the thinking itself is all that matters, is mistaken. Every masterthinker should know that the method in which his or her thinking is presented is of the utmost importance.

Let me make it quite clear that I am not suggesting that poor thinking presented in an attractive and slick fashion should be made to pass for good thinking. I am not suggesting that the skilled presentation skills of advertising should be used to disguise the poor quality of some thinking.

My emphasis on the importance of presentation is exactly the other way around. I am concerned that *good thinking may be lost because it is badly presented.*

PHYSICAL PRESENTATION

It is not my purpose here to go into all the details of physical presentation.

If written the material must be readable. The handwriting must be legible or typing must be used. There should be plenty of space between lines, between paragraphs, between sections and all around the page.

If something is densely presented it is often quite difficult to follow the thinking. Why this is so is less important than the tendency for it to be so. Unless paper shortage is a real problem allow as much space as possible.

If you are speaking, speak slowly and clearly. It is almost impossible to speak too slowly. You know your own ideas so you may be in a great hurry to pour them out. Your listener is not in the same position. What seems a normal pace for you may be much too fast for a listener - especially if you are trying to get across a number of ideas.

Try to change your tone and try to speak in paragraphs. There is nothing more difficult to understand than a long monotone. If you were presented with a page of densely-typed text with no paragraph breaks, you would find it difficult to follow the thinking. Yet many people speak in the same way.

In written material people can always go back to the beginning or go to the summary at the end. This is not the case with spoken material. So it is important to keep repeating the point that you are trying to make. It is also important to give summaries from time to time. You may feel this is unnecessary, a waste of time and even irritating to an audience. It is not.

CONCLUSIONS AND KEY POINTS

There are two possible approaches here.

The first approach is to start right out with the conclusions you are going to reach at the end. In some cases this may actually be a conclusion and in others it may be a number of key points. The key points would be the main points you are going to cover.

"In this piece I am going to show that lowering taxes will not increase employment."

"In this talk I am going to cover the following key points: the causes of unemployment; the effect of unemployment; the future of unemployment; and what we can do about unemployment."

We can sometimes go further. Many technical papers require that a summary of the piece be presented right at the beginning. The purpose behind this is that it would be a waste of time if someone had to read through a whole piece in order to find out whether that piece was relevant to what he or she wanted.

In general I would recommend this up-front presentation. Among other things it 'sets' or 'sensitizes' the mind of the listener so that he or she can better understand what is coming next. Without such a pre-setting the listener may wonder from moment-to-moment where the material is leading. Confusion can result if the listener makes a wrong assumption and sets off along a false track. There is nothing more difficult than trying to get someone off a false track.

The second possible approach is the exact opposite of the first approach.

If a detective book told you on the first page what was going to happen at the end, you would be very bored. If you went to the theatre and the actors told you in advance what was going to happen, you would feel cheated. In both cases the reason for the disappointment is that you want to see how things build up and develop.

So in this second style of presentation we start off with basic points. Then we gradually build up from these until we reach a conclusion.

It has to be said that this second method is much more difficult. We must know how to hold interest at every step. We must know how to develop a case and how to build up from basic points.

It is quite true that in education the teacher has some obligation to read the material that he or she has asked you to produce. This is certainly not the case in later life. No one has any obligation to read material without knowing where it is going to lead.

If you use this second method, you must be extremely careful to avoid confusion. As I have indicated, if the reader gets off onto the wrong track, then you have a disaster.

It should be said that if you are successful in all these things then the second method may be more powerful. This is because the reader (or listener) is led step-by-step to share your conclusion with you. In a sense you arrive at the conclusion hand-in-hand.

STRUCTURE

There are two basic types of structure: the tree type and the necklace type.

In the tree type of structure we have headings and subheadings and subsubheadings. It is important to get the organization of these different levels of headings very clear in one's mind. The classification networks mentioned in the section on 'nerves' can be of use here. The type style of the headings should indicate their level.

A much-used method of indicating headings and subheadings is to number them so that sub-subheading three of subheading two of major heading four would appear as: 4.2.3. This is the method used by lawyers for indicating paragraphs and subheadings of paragraphs.

I should enter a word of caution here. This sort of thing is very useful in legal documents because there is often a need to refer to some particular part of the text or even to argue about that part of the text. This need is not so strong in other areas. It can be very irritating if the thinker presents all his or her thinking as detailed headings and subheadings. It is much more natural to use broad headings and then to give the detail in narrative form (without further subdivision).

The necklace type of structure is quite different. In a necklace the beads are placed along the string one after another. They are all equally ranking. So in the necklace type of organization we have a number of paragraphs or sections which are all equally ranking. They just occur one after the other as with the beads in a necklace. No paragraph is a subdivision of another paragraph.

The necklace structure is very similar to the chapters in a book. The chapters are equal in rank (even if not equal in interest or importance). The two important things to keep in mind when using the necklace structure are:

1. Get the headings right.
2. Show clear separation between the sections.

It is important that the reader or the listener knows that a new section has been entered. The importance of getting the headings right arises from the need to parcel the material up into roughly comparable sections. There should be no section that is very much larger than the others - because it would then need breaking down into further sections.

It is permissible to use two layers of necklace in the sense that there may be the chapters in a book and within each chapter there may be another *necklace* of sections.

COMMUNICATION

You could present your thinking in an elegant form and then you might bury it in a stainless steel cylinder deep in the ground. Hundreds of years from now some archaeologist might discover your work. You might be writing a diary which is for your eyes alone - you might even instruct that it be burned when you are dead. Both these situations are rather unlikely. When you produce a piece of thinking it is usually for someone else to look at. Even if you are working alone on a project there is usually someone else involved somewhere along the way. So the concept of communication is important. Presentation by itself is only part of the concept of *skin*. Communication is the other part.

The essence of communication is that someone else is involved: You are trying to communicate with someone else.

It is important to keep that other person (or people) very clearly in mind. Thinking may be a selfish business, but *communication can never be a selfish business.* If it is selfish, then it is very poor communication.

In communication there are three important questions that you should constantly be asking yourself:

1. Why should the other person listen to you?
2. Where is the other person at?
3. What do you want from the communication?

It is astonishing how often communicators fail to keep these questions in mind.

Why should the other person listen to you? Because he or she is a tutor or teacher and that is part of his or her role? Because he or she is a parent and should therefore listen? That is about it. No one else is under any obligation to listen to you (unless perhaps you are injured in a criminal case). This is, of course, an exaggeration because you can always pay someone to listen to you: lawyer or doctor. The point I want to make is that there is no divine right to be heard.

So it is up to you to make that other person want to listen to you - and to go on listening. With *listening* I also include reading. An author has to make his or her book interesting enough to be read. A politician should make his or her speech interesting enough to be listened to. So if you want to he heard you have a duty to communicate.

That applies to the general case. In any particular case you should ask yourself the question: "Right now why does this person have to listen to me?" When you can keep that in mind you will become a good communicator.

The second question is also very important. It is no use using concepts and words which the other person cannot understand. You have to know *where the other person is at.* This is a broad way of saying that you have to get yourself inside the head of the other person.

There are two reasons for getting inside the head of the other person. The first reason is that you must understand the words, images and concepts which are available to the other person. There would be no point in talking French if the other person could understand only Italian. The second reason for getting inside the other person's head is to understand his or her motivation. The other person may like you, hate you or be neutral. If you are trying to persuade the other person about some matter, then you need to know where he or she stands.

EXERCISE -

You are a politician trying to explain that it is necessary to raise taxes. In a brief paragraph show how you would explain this to the following different people (repeat the paragraph in a different way for each).

1. *An enthusiastic supporter of your party.*
2. *A supporter of the opposing party.*
3. *A person of less than normal intelligence.*
4. *A highly intelligent person.*

EXERCISE -

Set down the motivation of the listener in each of the following cases.

1. *A woman discussing with her husband that they need more money to live on.*
2. *A salesman is trying to persuade a customer (woman) to buy a bigger car than she wants.*
3. *A person is being interviewed for a supervisory job in a factory.*
4. *A pupil is explaining to the teacher why he did not finish the assignment.*

We come now to the third of the three important questions. What is the purpose of your communication? The purpose of your thinking has already been considered in the section on *muscle* because muscle must always have a defined purpose. It may well be that the purpose of your thinking and the purpose of your communicating your thinking are exactly the same. This could be the case if you were part of a project team and you are explaining to the other members of the team what you think ought to be done.

There may be an occasion on which you are explaining some thinking of yours to a casual friend. Obviously you would not go into the detail required if you were explaining your thinking to a potential investor in your project.

If you are writing a sales brochure which is the more important: That you be as comprehensive as possible; or that you get the customer interested in your products?

EXERCISE

You think you have invented a new device which would stop cars from skidding on wet roads. You are talking about your invention to each of the different people listed below. Indicate the purpose of your communication in each case.

1. An engineer.
2. A potential investor in your product.
3. A friend.
4. Another inventor.
5. Your employer.

What do you want to end up with? What do you want the person to do or feel or know as a result of your communication?

It is not enough just to have a general sense of communication. You need to keep asking yourself the three basic questions again and again—on each specific occasion.

The biggest difficulty is that a thinker believes that he or she has finished the work when the thinking is done. Often this is not more than half the work. The other half of the work is communicating the results of the thinking to other people.

Skin: Summary

Skin has to do with appearance and presentation.

You have done your thinking. How do you present the results to other people?

If you do not take care with presentation, then the excellence of your thinking may be lost. No one is obliged to look through a poor presentation in order to find the hidden gold. So do not hide the gold: Present it well.

PHYSICAL PRESENTATION

There is order, neatness, tidiness and space when you are presenting something in the written form. If you are speaking, then you need to speak slowly and clearly and to break up your talk into sections. Even if it takes extra time, it is most important to produce a good presentation.

CONCLUSIONS AND KEY POINTS

When speaking you will need to insert frequent summaries and frequent repetition of the key points.

In general it is best to indicate what you are going to cover in the piece and even the conclusions that you are going to reach. This means setting out your conclusions and key points at the beginning. In a written piece you may even have a summary at the beginning.

If you wish to use the other method of starting from basic points and then taking the listener along with you to the conclusion, then you must be very careful that the listener or reader does not go astray through taking the wrong track. You must also be interesting enough to hold the attention of the listener or reader.

STRUCTURE

In the tree type of structure you will be using headings, subheadings and subsubheadings. Be very sure that you are both clear and consistent with your headings. Unless you are writing a legal document, do not overdo the levels of subheadings.

In the necklace type of structure you string equally ranking sections one after another as you might string beads on a necklace. Try to choose headings which will give sections of roughly equal size. Be very sure to show when a section has ended. Occasionally - as in a book - each of the sections may include another necklace of smaller sections.

COMMUNICATION

Always remember that communication involves another person or other people. You have to keep the other party very clearly in mind. It is not like putting a notice up on a board and then hoping that someone will read that notice. You have to be trying to communicate with the other party all the time.

You need to be clear why you are communicating: What do you hope to achieve? You need to know why the other person should bother to listen. You need to get inside the head of the other person in order to use appropriate words and images and in order to understand the motivation of that other person. These things are summed up in the following key questions:

1. Why should the other person listen to you?
2. Where is the other person at?
3. What do you want from the communication?

You should keep these questions in mind in general. You should also repeat them to yourself on every occasion when you are communicating the results of your thinking.

Remember that it is the *skin* which is seen by the world outside you.

Health

The most important thing about the human body is that it should be healthy.

Using the *body frame* idiom for thinking means that we should be interested in the *health* of our thinking.

When we talk about health we talk about weaknesses, deficiencies, dangers and even poisons. We can apply some of these same words to thinking. What is the weakness of this thinking? What is the danger of this thinking?

At this last stage in BFT we put everything together and have an overall look at the thinking. In an active thinking situation we have a look at the thinking we have produced. In a reactive thinking situation we have a look at the thinking that is being put before us - and we also have a look at our thinking about this.

In the BFT method, *health* stands for evaluation. We set out to evaluate the thinking.

MUSCLE AND EVALUATION

The section on *muscle* is also a section on evaluation. When we set out to assess the *muscle* of a piece of thinking (our own or someone else's) we are evaluating its power or force. If we find that it has no power, then it means that the thinking is weak, ineffective or wrong. When we ask: What is the power of thinking, we are also asking, what is the value of this thinking?

Because of the importance of evaluation, we are going to take another look at evaluation in this section on *health.* Some of the things we shall be looking at here will overlap with things that were done in the muscle section.

The points of view of this section and the muscle section are different. In the muscle section we look specifically at the power of the thinking - and at the source of that power. In this section we take an over-all view: What is the health of the thinking?

ACTIVE THINKING

You are thinking about some project. You have to make a choice or a decision. You need to know if your choice or plan of action is valid. You need to carry out an evaluation.

The two key questions are:

1. Is it good in itself?
2. Is it good for me?

The answers to those two questions will provide the evaluation of any piece of active thinking.

GOOD IN ITSELF

Will the idea work? Could it work for anyone? Is the idea sound? These sorts of questions are asked about the idea or plan *itself.* There is no reference to the person who is going to follow the plan or choice. For example, a perpetual motion machine will not work for anyone. It is wrong in itself.

We can ask a series of questions to determine whether an idea is good in itself:

1. Is it based on information or known facts?
2. Is it based on personal experience or the experience of others?
3. Is it logically derived from known facts or known experience?
4. What are the risks and dangers?
5. What are the detailed consequences of putting this idea into action?

The last question is the most important. We run the action suggestion forward in our minds in order to see all the consequences. If you want to evaluate a route on a map, you follow it through to see if it gets you to your destination. You also see the terrain it passes through and the dangers. So the assessment of consequences is the crucial evaluation procedure.

GOOD FOR ME

The idea may be very good in itself, but it may not be any good for me (or the thinker). Working on an oil drilling rig may bring in lots of money, but the thinker may not have the physical size and strength to do such work. So now we have to look at the *fit* between idea itself and the person who is going to have to use it. Is the idea a good idea for me?

We can again ask a number of questions:

1. Does it fit my purpose, my needs and my wants?
2. Does it fit my priorities?
3. Does it fit my values and principles?
4. Does it fit my resources (time, money etc.)?
5. Does it fit my self-image?

It follows that in order to answer these questions the masterthinker is forced to spell out needs, wants, priorities, values, resources, etc.

The most important thing about making a choice or decision is *to know why you have made it.* If a decision feels right and you can spell out why you are making it, then that decision is right. Later on you may find that it does not work out as you had hoped. This does not mean that you made the wrong decision. It means that things did not work out as you had supposed. Given your knowledge and your feelings, the decision was right at the time.

EXERCISE -

Answer both sets of questions (good in itself, good for me) on behalf of the following people and the indicated decisions.

1. *A senior IBM executive, aged 45, decides to leave the large corporation to set up his own business which will be to supply computer software. He has no direct experience in this area, but believes that he can hire the necessary talent.*

2. *A brilliant woman lawyer decides to postpone having children for the first ten years of her career in order to give her a chance of establishing her position.*

3. *An investor decides to put quite a lot of money into a new invention that claims to get cars to run on a mixture of gasoline and water.*

4. *A student notices that another student has been stealing and decides to report this to the authorities.*

REACTIVE THINKING

When we react to thinking that is put before us we use the *muscle* type of assessment. If we start off from the assumption that the thinking has no value or force, we can then try to see how the *muscle* of that particular piece of thinking is built up: Is it information muscle? Is it logic muscle? Is it emotional muscle?

As with evaluation in active thinking we can ask a series of questions:

1. What is the muscle here?
2. What is the purpose of the thinker?
3. What is my purpose?
4. What are the consequences of my reaction to this thinking, for example, if I accept it?
5. How do the underlying information, assumptions, values and emotions, fit with mine?

Note that the question concerning muscle already covers such matters as the information or logical base of the argument. In active thinking a close look at the consequences of accepting a line of action is very important. Even in reactive thinking we need to look closely at the consequences of accepting a line of argument.

In reactive thinking we are much concerned with such questions as: Is it true or false? Is it wrong or right? Does it make sense?

In reactive thinking we must always be aware that something may indeed make sense *once we accept certain basic assumptions or values.*

"If I accepted those assumptions of yours then I would accept your conclusion."

"If I accepted those values of yours then I would accept your conclusion - but I have different values."

This is a very important point to remember. A line of thinking may be logically consistent and therefore *right* in itself. But it may be based on a value system that the listener neither shares nor accepts. The thinker should spell this out very carefully.

EXERCISE -

Give your reaction to the following line of argument. Refer to the muscle section if you wish.

"If a surgeon makes a mistake, he or she can be sued for huge amounts of money (even millions of dollars). To cover this possibility surgeons have to pay huge insurance premiums. Now a surgeon's mistakes can be very serious and can be a matter of life and death or permanent incapacity, so it is only right that surgeons should be heavily penalized for making mistakes. It is also right that the victims should be compensated. It is also true that lawyers inflate the claims because they get a share of the award and can often make hundreds of thousands of dollars out of someone's misfortune. This is also fair; otherwise victims would not be able to afford to sue. Surgeons claim that they are only human and that some mistakes must occur. In some cases, surgeons have refused to carry out certain types of operations because the risks are too high. So the patient suffers. To deal with this problem, some states have passed laws that put a limit on the amount of damages that are payable. This seems a fair solution."

EXERCISE -

Taking the background of the former situation (medical liability) give your reaction to the proposal given below.

"One solution would be for the patient, himself or herself, to buy insurance before an operation. It is rather like buying your own insurance when you get on a plane or get into a car. You are taking the risk and if you want compensation it is up to you to buy the insurance. If you want a lot of compensation, then you must pay a high premium. For those who could not afford to pay such premiums, there would be standard insurance which the doctor would carry - but with a limit on damages."

EXERCISE -

Give your reaction to the following line of thinking:

"Good pupils are always able to look after themselves. They will always do well in exams and later on in life. So it would make far more sense to use the best teachers with the poorer pupils. These are the ones who really need help. This is where help could really make a difference to the whole career and after life of a pupil. These are the pupils who are bored with school. If a good teacher could excite their interest, then that could make a dramatic difference. So there should be a deliberate policy of putting the best teachers with the less able students. Perhaps not with the poorest students because it may not be possible to make much difference here, but at least with the borderline ones."

Health:
Summary

In the BFT method *health* refers to the over-all evaluation of the thinking.

Is the thinking weak?

Is the thinking deficient?

Is the thinking dangerous?

Is the thinking wrong?

So we do a *health scan* on the thinking. We check it out at various points.

MUSCLE AND HEALTH

There is overlap between assessing the muscle of the thinking and doing a health scan. In the muscle idiom we look for the force or power of the thinking. We may find that it is weak or absent. We may find that what seems to be strength is only an illusion because it is incorrectly based. The health scan should include all this and go beyond it. For example, the thinking may be powerful in itself, but not suited for the thinker to act upon.

ACTIVE THINKING

Here the thinker is having to make a choice or decision or is having to set up some action plan in connection with a project (or problem). Evaluation is very important.

There are two key questions to be asked:

1. Is it good in itself?
2. Is it good for me?

In assessing whether the idea is good in itself we look at its basis in fact or experience. We look at the logic of the idea. We assess the risks and dangers.

In assessing any idea in active thinking the most important thing is to run the idea forward in time and to watch what happens.

Even if the idea is good and viable in itself, we then need to see if it fits the person or persons who are going to have to act upon it. Is there a fit with purpose, needs, wants, priorities, values, principles, etc. Even if there is good fit with all of these, we need to see if the idea fits the available resources: money, time, energy, people, etc.

The most important point is to be very clear as to why a certain decision or choice is made. If you can really spell this out, then you are likely to make the right decision.

REACTIVE THINKING

The evaluation in reactive thinking applies both to the material put before the thinker and also to his or her thinking about this. In reactive thinking the evaluation is based on the 'muscle' idiom. We look for the power basis of the argument. If we find none, then we can dismiss the thinking.

In addition to this direct muscle assessment we also need to go a little more broadly to consider the consequences of accepting the line of argument—or of dismissing it. How does it affect us? What are our purposes? What is the purpose of the presenter of the material?

In reactive thinking it is particularly important to pay attention to assumptions and values. It is perfectly possible for a line of argument to be correct in itself - provided that the listener accepts the same values and assumptions as the presenter.

So the two key questions could be:

1. What is the muscle here?
2. What are the values and assumptions?

OUTCOME

When doing a health scan you have to be happy in your mind that the thinking is *healthy.* If you have any doubts at all then you must do further checks - as the doctor would.